Change-mapping

Connecting business tools to manage change

"Change-mapping sets out a focused and practical framework and set of best practices that take the reader step by step through the process of affecting a change. This book is a 'keeper' and will be taking place on my shelf that will keep it within easy reach."
Neil Kemp, Lead Enterprise Architect, Shared Services Canada

"This is a book for all the enterprise architects, change managers and management consultants who want to level up their game beyond the ubiquitous business model canvas."
Jan Rautenkranc , Business Architect, ČSOB

Tom Graves with Joseph Chittenden

Published by
Tetradian Books
Unit 215
Communications House
9 St Johns Street
Colchester
Essex
CO2 7NN
England

http://www.tetradianbooks.com

First published January 2020
ISBN 978-1-906681-40-1 (Paperback)
ISBN 978-1-906681-41-8 (Ebook)
First Edition

Contents

Part 1: What is *Change-mapping?*

Part 2: The basic *Change-mapping tool-sheets*

Part 3: Advanced Change-mapping in brief

Preface
The inspiration behind the book

A few years back, a friend turned up at my house, looking frazzled and frustrated. He'd been trying to rethink his business-model, he said, waving various business tool-sheets. *"How do I use these?"*, he asked. *"I've filled in all the tool-sheets, but they don't tell me anything useful! It's like looking in a mirror, it doesn't tell me anything I don't already know. What can I do, to make it make sense? How do I link all these tools together?"*

We set to work. It didn't take long: in not much more than an hour, he had the basis for his new business-model, with new services, new products and new ways of working, all built upon what he already had. We'd used much the same tools as he'd brought with him; but what made the difference was how we'd used them - a structured way to map out the changes that he'd need, and how they would work in practice. A week later, he called again, saying that the insights had kept on coming for him throughout the following days: a new logo, a new website, a new set of services that he could offer his clients. Everything worked together now, he said, excitedly; everything made sense. And it's still going well for him now.

Fact is there's no shortage of tools and techniques, for almost any purpose, in business and beyond. But what's often been lacking is a good way to use them, to get them to work well, together, fast, across every context, every scope, every scale. A way that has the power and versatility to tackle any question or concern, to any depth, a way that lines up with how experts actually work, a way that works with almost any tool, yet is still simple enough for anyone to use.

That's the challenge we set out to resolve with *Change-mapping*.
And that's what you have in your hands right now. We hope you find it useful.

Tom Graves
Colchester, England
February 2020

A big thank you!
To our co-creators and valued patrons

This book would not have existed without a large amount of people who over the years have contributed great amounts of time and money to bring *Change-mapping* to a wider audience. The author would like to thank:

Michael Smith (Mexico)
Helena Read (Australia)

Patrons

The author would also like to thank all the valued Patrons at *www.patreon.com/tetradian* who helped fund the production of this book.
As well they have given excellent feedback and helped with testing the materials.

How you can get involved!
To find out more about Change-mapping visit:
www. changemappingbook.com

www.patreon.com/ tetradian
If you would like to be involved with the development of new tools, testing and more then head over to Patreon to get involved.

About the author
Tom Graves

Tom is known as a highly innovative thought leader on the futures of business. With a keen eye for systems and structure, he has nearly 40 years experience in knowledge management, skills research and software development. He is a prolific author, and experienced presenter on radio and television, at conferences and in workshops and seminars.
Contact: info@tetradian.com

About the designer
Joseph Chittenden

Joseph has produced concepts and visuals for companies such as: *Tesco, Lotus sports cars, T-Mobile, Honda, Makita, HM The Cabinet Office, Superdrug/3Phones,* and others on behalf of design agencies in England and Dubai.
www.jc3dvis.co.uk

How to use this book
Getting the most out of the book

Change-mapping uses a simple framework and tool-sheets to help your organisation to explore or resolve an issue affected by change.

If your organisation has an issue which needs to be explored or resolved, then *Change-mapping* can be used to map out what is known and what is not.

This book shows how a small team can explore or resolve an issue from the wider context down to the fine detail. You will see how a basic *Change-mapping* mission works, step by step and with worked examples. In addition there is :

A trouble shooting section. A section showing the tools in action. A complete set of basic tool-sheets for use within *Change-mapping*.

As well as a brief introduction to some of the more advanced methods available.

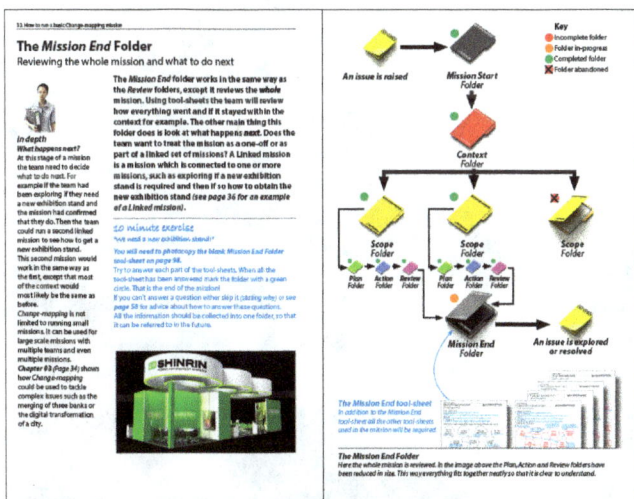

Change-mapping breaks down how to map change facing organisations. Each chapter has an explanation of a key point, simple exercises and diagrams.

Part 1:
What is *Change-mapping?*

Introducing *Change-mapping* and how to use it to explore or resolve issues affected by change.

Chapter 1: Introducing *Change-mapping*

Asking the right questions to find the right answers

In depth

While there are many existing business tools it can be difficult to connect different ones together to produce a cohesive picture of a change issue.

Change-mapping works by using a simple scalable framework of folders. Each folder explores or resolves and issue at a certain level of detail. Inside each folder the users can use basic tool-sheets to explore or resolve an issue. If the basic tool-sheets don't provide enough information then more advanced pre-existing tools can be plugged in.

This means that *Change-mapping* can adapt to any issue of any size.

In this chapter we show the building blocks of *Change-mapping*, a system designed to map issues affected by change.

We see why there is a need for *Change-mapping* and introduce missions. *Missions* are like projects in that they tackle an issue except that they can be made up of many projects.

We will also see who does what in a mission introducing *Pathfinders*, *Observers* and *Explorers* who all have distinct roles in a mission.

As well we introduce *tool-sheets* which are used to gather ideas, information and insights about an issue affected by change.

How to use Change-mapping

General instructions

Have a quick flick through this chapter to become familiar with the main parts of *Change-mapping*.

Then look at **Chapter 2** *(page 18)* to see a simple *Change-mapping* mission in action and then refer back to this chapter to confirm certain details.

In addition try the exercises in this chapter to explore the simplest parts of *Change-mapping*.

missions and use it in other missions.

Change-mapping can also accommodate much larger missions with more complex issues.

See **Chapter 12** for more about different types of missions.

30 minute exercise

The issue is: "*Shinrin needs a new exhibition stand!*" Assemble a small team, one will be the *Pathfinder**, one will be the *Observer** and the rest will be the *Explorers**.

Run the simplified mission *(see right)* to see why *Shinrin* might need a new exhibition stand. Each folder has a question *(blue text)* which needs to be answered. When the question has been answered move to the next folder.

Basic *Change-mapping* works in the same way except that instead of only one question per folder, there are many questions which are on tool-sheets.

Chapter 02 shows how to run a basic *Change-mapping* mission, with every step shown.

*For more about team members see page 10.

A typical response to change
Rushing to find a solution

In depth
When faced with change a typical response is to rush to solve it with a plan and then enact the plan. Rushing to find a solution (or solutioneering, as it is often called) can have the potential for extremely costly and even dangerous outcomes for those involved.

Working with change is itself a skill, an organisation's processes can change once it better understands how to manage change and the unknown.

"*Change is the only constant*" to quote the ancient Greek philosopher *Heraclitus**. Change can often instil panic where an issue requires solving. For example a CEO states "We need a new exhibition stand!" So his team rushes to plan how to build the stand and then has it built. This all seems fine but did anyone stop to ask "*Why do we need a new stand?*" What if it turned out that an exhibition stand was not the best solution? Another problem can be rushing to a solution which makes it difficult to coordinate between different teams who need immediate access to changing information.

While there are different systems to deal with these issues, they can be too complicated or context dependent. This book describes a new more structured approach to mapping change.
* https://en.wikiquote.org/wiki/Heraclitus

10 minute exercise
The issue is: "we need to re-brand the Shinrin organisation!" You have five minutes to think how you would tackle this issue. You may have thought of a rough plan about how to re-brand an organisation.

For the last five minutes ask questions about *why* a re-brand is required and if there may be better solutions than just a re-brand.

Should we change this colour to red?

森林 SHINRIN
FOREST MANAGEMENT SYSTEMS

Does the logo work well on social media?

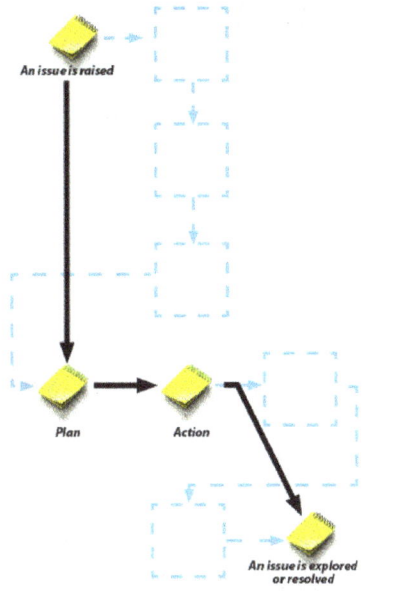

An issue is raised

Plan

Action

An issue is explored or resolved

A typical approach to change
While this approach may work, it misses important steps, such as asking "Why does the issue need resolving".

Introducing *Change-mapping* missions
Are you exploring or resolving an issue?

In depth
Missions can be stand-alone missions or part of a set of linked missions. *Linked missions* take information from linked missions and use it in other missions. *Change-mapping* can also accommodate much larger missions with more complex issues. See Chapter 12 for more about different types of missions.

Change-mapping uses missions to explore or resolve an issue affected by change.

An important thing to note is what *type* of mission you are planning to do. Are you trying to **explore** or **resolve** an issue? It might seem obvious that a mission will be to resolve an issue. But before running a mission to resolve an issue typically a mission is run to confirm why it needs changing. Doing this can sometimes reveal that the issue doesn't need changing or maybe it needs changing in a different way to originally imagined.

30 minute exercise
The issue is: "Shinrin needs a new exhibition stand!" Assemble a small team, one will be the *Pathfinder**, one will be the *Observer** and the rest will be the *Explorers**. Run the simplified mission (see right) to see why Shinrin might need a new exhibition stand. Each folder has a question (blue text) which needs to be answered. When the question has been answered move to the next folder.

Basic *Change-mapping* works in the same way except that instead of only one question per folder, there are many questions which are on tool-sheets.

Chapter 02 shows how to run a basic *Change-mapping* mission, with every step shown.
*For more about team members see page 10.

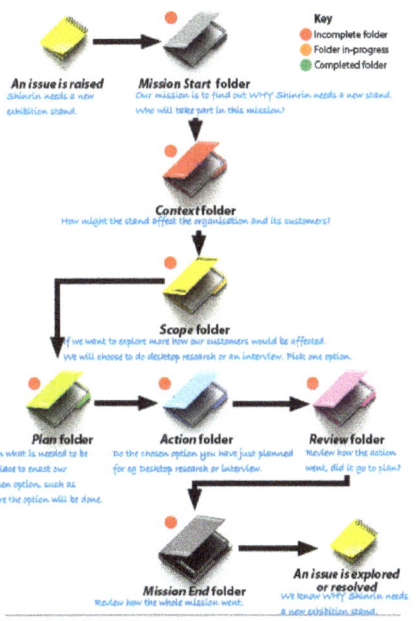

SHINRIN

Key
- Incomplete folder
- Folder in-progress
- Completed folder

An issue is raised
Shinrin needs a new exhibition stand.

Mission Start folder
Our mission is to find out WHY Shinrin needs a new stand. Who will take part in this mission?

Context folder
How might the stand affect the organisation and its customers?

Scope folder
If we want to explore more how our customers would be affected. We will choose to do desktop research or an interview. Pick one option.

Plan folder
Plan what is needed to be in place to enact our chosen option, such as where the option will be done.

Action folder
Do the chosen option you have just planned for eg desktop research or interview.

Review folder
Review how the action went, did it go to plan?

Mission End folder
Review how the whole mission went.

An issue is explored or resolved
We know WHY Shinrin needs a new exhibition stand.

A simplified change-mapping mission
This forms part of a 30 minute exercise (see left) to become familiar with what each folder does in Change-mapping missions.

This chapter introduces the main parts of Change-mapping.

A typical response to change
Rushing to find a solution

In depth
When faced with change a typical response is to rush to solve it with a plan and then enact the plan.

Rushing to find a solution *(or solutioneering, as it is often called)* can have the potential for extremely costly and even dangerous outcomes for those involved.

Working with change is itself a skill, an organisation's processes can change once it better understands how to manage change and the unknown.

"Change is the only constant" to quote the ancient Greek philosopher *Heraclitus**. Change can often instil panic where an issue requires solving. For example a CEO states "We need a new exhibition stand!" So his team rushes to plan how to build the stand and then has it built. This all seems fine but did anyone stop to ask *"Why do we need a new stand?"* What if it turned out that an exhibition stand was not the best solution? Another problem can be rushing to a solution which makes it difficult to coordinate between different teams who need immediate access to changing information.

While there are different systems to deal with these issues, they can be too complicated or context dependent. This book describes a new more structured approach to mapping change.

* https://en.wikiquote.org/wiki/Heraclitus

10 minute exercise
The issue is: "We need to re-brand the Shinrin organisation!" You have five minutes to think how you would tackle this issue. Use this time to think of a rough plan about how to re-brand an organisation.

For the last five minutes ask questions about *why* a re-brand is required and if there may be better solutions than just a re-brand.

Should we change this colour to red?

森林 **SHINRIN**
FOREST MANAGEMENT SYSTEMS

Does the logo work well on social media?

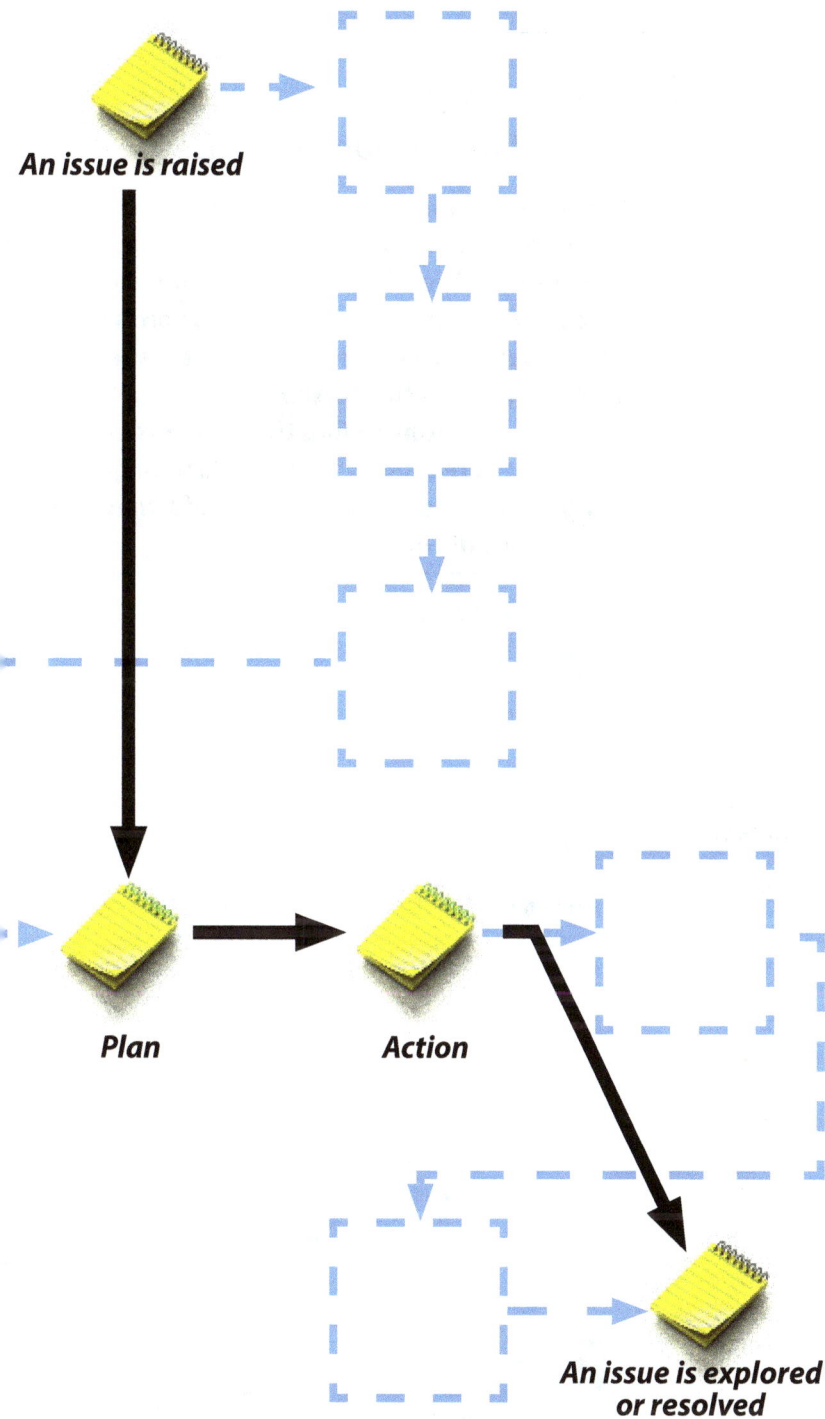

An issue is raised

Plan

Action

An issue is explored or resolved

A typical approach to change
While this approach may work, it misses important steps, such as asking "Why does the issue need resolving".

Introducing *Change-mapping*

Asking the right questions to find the right answers

Change-mapping uses a structured approach to guide change. The system works by taking a small team of people and running a *Mission* to explore or resolve a change issue. Each mission is split into folders. Each folder looks at the issue from a certain perspective to allow your team to ask the right questions to find the right answers. In each folder are a set of tool-sheets with questions designed to help you gain ideas, information and insights about the issue.

In depth

The core method of *Change-mapping* is to break any issue into manageable sections which can be examined in the amount of detail required. These sections *(shown as folders)* are: ***Context, Scope, Plan, Action*** and ***Review***. All of these folders are wrapped up in a ***Mission Start*** and a ***Mission End***, to help you keep track of everything.

Each folder depends on the others, because information found will flow up and down between the folders as you find out more about the issue and then how to solve it. *Change-mapping* is not a rigid step by step. At each stage you check that you are not moving out of context or creeping out of scope. This also avoids plans that are hopelessly out of touch with the real world.

10 minute exercise

The issue is: "We need to re-brand the Shinrin organisation!" Briefly look at the diagram on the right and imagine how you might approach the re-brand exercise by splitting the issue into parts. In the **Mission Start** folder state if the mission is to explore or resolve the issue. In the **Context** folder set the issue in context. In the **Scope** folder pick one part which is unclear to explore or resolve further.

In the **Plan** folder plan how to explore or resolve it further in broad detail. In the **Action** folder enact the plan. In the **Review** folder review how that proceeded. And lastly in the **Mission End** folder review if the whole very simple mission achieved what was stated in the **Mission Start** folder. This is a highly simplified version of a *Change-mapping* mission, the next page shows in more detail how missions work.

What is wrong with the current branding, why does it need changing?

森林 **SHINRIN**
FOREST MANAGEMENT SYSTEMS

What is the evidence that the logo needs changing?

An issue is raised

Mission Start folder
*Setup a mission to resolve
or explore the issue*

Context folder
Set the issue in context

Scope folder
*Explore options for action to explore
or resolve unclear parts of the issue*

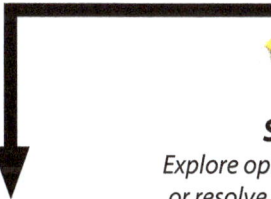

Plan folder
*Plan how to explore or
resolve parts of the issue*

Action folder
*Enact the plan to explore or
resolve parts of the issue*

Review folder
*Review if the plan was
enacted successfully*

Mission End folder
Review the whole mission

**An issue is explored
or resolved**

Key
● Incomplete folder
● Folder in-progress
● Completed folder

A more structured approach to change
*Change-mapping breaks a change issue into folders, these sections are linked by a pathway
(black arrows) and a simple signalling system (coloured circles).*

Introducing *Change-mapping* missions
Are you exploring or resolving an issue?

In depth

Missions can be stand-alone missions or part of a set of linked missions. *Linked missions* take information from linked missions and use it in other missions. *Change-mapping* can also accommodate much larger missions with more complex issues. See **Chapter 12** for more about different types of missions.

Change-mapping uses missions to explore or resolve an issue affected by change.
An important thing to note is what *type* of mission you are planning to do. Are you trying to **explore** or **resolve** an issue? It might seem obvious that a mission will be to resolve an issue. But before running a mission to resolve an issue typically a mission is run to confirm why it needs changing. Doing this can sometimes reveal that the issue doesn't need changing or maybe it needs changing in a different way to originally imagined.

30 minute exercise

The issue is: "Shinrin needs a new exhibition stand!"
Assemble a small team, one will be the **Pathfinder***, one will be the **Observer*** and the rest will be the **Explorers***.
Run the simplified mission *(see right)* to see why *Shinrin* might need a new exhibition stand. Each folder has a question *(blue text)* which needs to be answered. When the question has been answered move to the next folder.
Basic **Change-mapping** works in the same way except that instead of only one question per folder, there are many questions which are on tool-sheets.
Chapter 02 shows how to run a basic **Change-mapping** mission, with every step shown.
*For more about team members see page 12.

Key

- 🔴 Incomplete folder
- 🟠 Folder in-progress
- 🟢 Completed folder

An issue is raised
Shinrin needs a new exhibition stand.

Mission Start folder
Our mission is to find out WHY Shinrin needs a new stand. Who will take part in this mission?

Context folder
How might the stand affect the organisation and its customers?

Scope folder
If we want to explore more how our customers would be affected. We will choose to do desktop research or an interview. Pick one option.

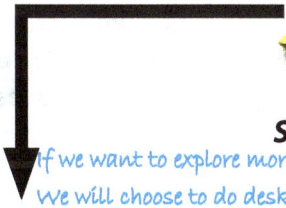

Plan folder
Plan what is needed to be in place to enact our chosen option, such as where the option will be done.

Action folder
Do the chosen option you have just planned for eg Desktop research or interview.

Review folder
Review how the action went, did it go to plan?

Mission End folder
Review how the whole mission went.

An issue is explored or resolved
We know WHY Shinrin needs a new exhibition stand.

A simplified change-mapping mission
This forms part of a 30 minute exercise (see left) to become familiar with what each folder does in Change-mapping missions.

Who does what in a mission

The different roles in a basic *Change-mapping* mission

In depth
Are there any other roles?
*The roles described here should be all that's needed for a basic change-mapping mission. When the missions increase in size and complexity more specialised roles are likely to be required. These are discussed in brief in **Part 03**, they include:*
Librarians, *whose tasks include archiving, storing and distributing information between missions.*
Coordinators, *whose tasks include coordinating who does what and when during single and multiple missions.*
Architects, *who coordinate multiple missions at the same time.*

A *Change-mapping* mission is used to explore or resolve an issue affected by change. A mission will be created to respond to an issue.
An issue might be raised by a member of staff, a client or potentially anyone. The *Issue Raiser* could also be the *Decision Maker* who will decide what to do based on what is found in the mission.
In basic *Change-mapping* missions there is a *Mission Commander* who manages the mission, but doesn't offer insights. Next there is a *Pathfinder* who again doesn't offer insights but keeps the mission on track. There is also an *Observer* who records insights but doesn't offer them. The last main role is the *Explorer*. In basic missions there can be four to twelve *Explorers*. Their main task is to gather insights, ideas and information. If everyone is an *Explorer* a mission can descend into chaos with no insights being captured and recorded.

10 minute exercise
"Smart-watch failing in cold conditions"
Gather ideas about why a smart-watch might fail in cold conditions. Have one person, the *Observer*, dedicated to capturing ideas. The others will generate ideas, with the *Pathfinder* making sure the exercise stays on task.
After five minutes have the *Observer* read what was found. For the last few minutes decide areas which might need more information.

Issue Raiser
Number of people:
1+
Duties:
The **Issue Raiser** can be a member of the organisation, a stakeholder or potentially anyone. They can sometimes also be the **Decision Maker**. They bring the issue to the attention of the **Decision Maker** who if required will then set up a mission to explore or resolve the issue.

Decision Maker
Number of people:
1+
Duties:
The **Decision Maker** most likely will not take part in missions. They often will set up the mission and decide if a mission is required. They may also report to the **Issue Raiser** if required about what will happen post-mission.

Mission Commander
Number of people:
1
Duties:
The **Mission Commander** monitors how the mission is proceeding and has the final say if no one else can decide what to do next. They most likely will report to the **Decision Maker** about what is found.

Pathfinder
Number of people:
1
Duties:
Keep the mission on track while allowing unexpected ideas, information and insights to be captured by the **Explorers**.
They assist with choosing and using tool-sheets*.
They do not offer ideas, insights and information about the issue.

Observer
Number of people:
1
Duties:
Write down the ideas, information and insights the **Explorers** find while using the tool-sheets* during a mission.
They do not offer ideas, insights and information about the issue.

Explorers
Number of people:
4-12
Duties:
Using tool-sheets* capture ideas, information and insights about the issue, which the mission is trying to **explore** or **resolve**.

For information about tool-sheets see page 16.

The main roles in basic Change-mapping
The image above shows the main roles in basic Change-mapping.

How to set up a mission
What your team will need to successfully run a mission

In depth
The mission shown in detail on **page 18** is a simplified example of a basic mission. This allows the new user to see how everything works rather than overloading them with information.
As you become familiar with all the parts that make up *Change-mapping* more parts will be introduced. *Change-mapping* has been designed to used on any issue of any size or complexity.
These larger and more complex missions and how *Change-mapping* can be used on them is described in **Chapter 3** and also **Chapter 12**.

Basic *Change-mapping* missions are quick to setup *(see below)*. Each mission has a dedicated *Mission Start* folder with two tool-sheets *(see right)* which are used to set up the mission by posing questions such as: What is the issue, Who is involved and other similar questions.
Most probably the most important things needed to set up a mission are:
An issue which needs to explored or resolved.
A decision whether to explore or resolve the issue.

How to set up a basic mission
General instructions
You will need:

4-12 Explorers* to capture ideas, information and insights during a mission.

1 Pathfinder* who will make sure the Explorers stay on the task, while allowing unexpected insights to occur.

1 Observer* who will note down all the teams findings on the tool-sheets and additional paper if required.

Photocopies of the blank tool-sheets. See **Part 2** *(page 60)* for a selection of basic tool-sheets. You will need at least one set of the tool-sheets from each of the seven folders.

An issue which needs to be explored or resolved.

A dedicated area for the mission to be conducted.

Additional pens and paper

*See page 12 for more details about the roles in Change-mapping.

Plan basic tool-sheet 1 of 2 ① CHANGE-MAPPING

General information

Mission identification:
Shimrin/0001/2.2.22/new exhibition stand enquiry
Sheet identification:
Shimrin/0001/2.2.22/new exhibition stand enquiry, Plan basic tool-sheet 1
The issue is:
Marketing manager believes we should invest in a new exhibition stand.
Our mission is:
To confirm to the board that we should invest in a new exhibition stand.
This Scope folder explores or resolves which part of the issue?
Look at what our competitors are doing to promote their products.
This Plan tool-sheet is used to plan?
Setup a meeting with Beta company for information.

Are these in place before the plan is enacted?

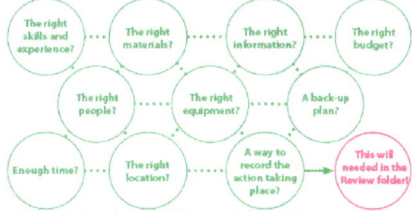

- **The right skills and experience?** The task seems not too specialised.
- **The right materials?** We think so.
- **The right information?** We could do this, but should meet question list.
- **The right budget?** The budget seems fine.
- **The right people?** Bring in some of the marketing team.
- **The right equipment?** Laptop, wifi, pen and paper.
- **A back-up plan?** Yes, but we have sufficient time to explore other options.
- **Enough time?** It should be sufficient time.
- **The right location?** Our offices.
- **A way to record the action taking place?** Will take notes on how process went.
- **This will needed in the Review folder!**

How might these be avoided when enacting the plan?

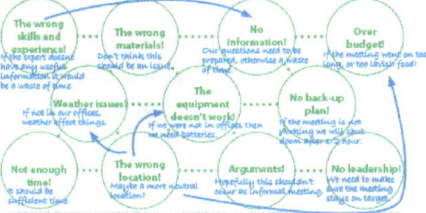

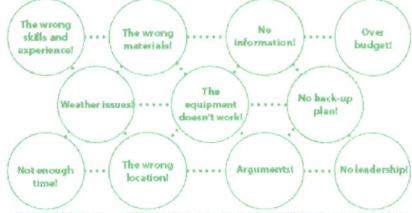

- **The wrong skills and experience?** If the expert doesn't have any useful information, it would be a waste of time.
- **The wrong materials?** Don't think this should be an issue.
- **No information!** Our questions need to be prepared, otherwise a waste of time.
- **Over budget!** If the meeting went on too long, or too lavish food!
- **Weather issues!** If not in our offices, weather effect things.
- **The equipment doesn't work!** If we were not in offices then we need batteries.
- **No back-up plan!** If the meeting is not working we will just about after ½ hour.
- **Not enough time!** It should be sufficient time.
- **The wrong location!** Maybe a more neutral location!
- **Arguments!** Hopefully this shouldn't occur as informal meeting.
- **No leadership!** We need to make sure the meeting stays on track.

Plan basic tool-sheet 1 of 2 ① CHANGE-MAPPING

General information

Mission identification:

Sheet identification:

The issue is:

Our mission is:

This Scope folder explores or resolves which part of the issue?

This Plan tool-sheet is used to plan?

Are these in place before the plan is enacted?

- The right skills and experience?
- The right materials?
- The right information?
- The right budget?
- The right people?
- The right equipment?
- A back-up plan?
- Enough time?
- The right location?
- A way to record the action taking place?
- This will needed in the Review folder!

How might these be avoided when enacting the plan?

- The wrong skills and experience?
- The wrong materials!
- No information!
- Over budget!
- Weather issues!
- The equipment doesn't work!
- No back-up plan!
- Not enough time!
- The wrong location!
- Arguments!
- No leadership!

Review basic tool-sheet ① CHANGE-MAPPING

General information

Mission identification:
Shimrin/0001/2.2.22/new exhibition stand enquiry
Sheet identification:
Shimrin/0001/2.2.22/new exhibition stand enquiry, Review basic tool-sheet
The issue is:
Marketing manager believes we should invest in a new exhibition stand.
Our mission is:
To confirm to the board that we should invest in a new exhibition stand.
The Scope folder explored or resolved which part of the issue?
Look at what our competitors are doing to promote their products.
The accompanying Plan tool-sheet was used to plan?
Setup a meeting with Beta company for information.

How did the enactment of the task differ from the plan? Was there...

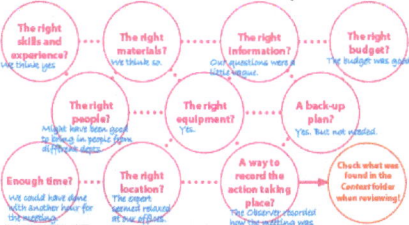

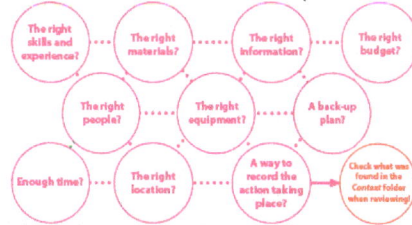

- **The right skills and experience?** We think yes
- **The right materials?** We think so.
- **The right information?** Our questions were a little vague.
- **The right budget?** The budget was good.
- **The right people?** Might have been good to bring in people from different depts.
- **The right equipment?** Yes.
- **A back-up plan?** Yes. But not needed.
- **Enough time?** We could have done with another hour for the meeting.
- **The right location?** The expert seemed relaxed at our offices.
- **A way to record the action taking place?** The Observer recorded how the meeting was conducted.
- **Check what was found in the Context folder when reviewing!**

What was the outcome of the task enactment?

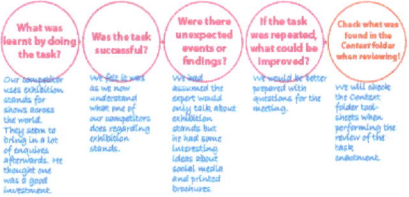

- **What was learnt by doing the task?** Our competitor uses exhibition stands for shows across the world. They seem to bring in a lot of enquiries afterwards. He thought one was a good investment.
- **Was the task successful?** We felt it was as we now understand what one of our competitors does regarding exhibition stands.
- **Were there unexpected events or findings?** We had assumed the expert would only talk about exhibition stands but he had some interesting ideas about social media and printed brochures.
- **If the task was repeated, what could be improved?** We would be better prepared with questions for the meeting.
- **Check what was found in the Context folder when reviewing!**

Review basic tool-sheet ① CHANGE-MAPPING

General information

Mission identification:

Sheet identification:

The issue is:

Our mission is:

The Scope folder explored or resolved which part of the issue?

The accompanying Plan tool-sheet was used to plan?

How did the enactment of the task differ from the plan? Was there...

- The right skills and experience?
- The right materials?
- The right information?
- The right budget?
- The right people?
- The right equipment?
- A back-up plan?
- Enough time?
- The right location?
- A way to record the action taking place?
- Check what was found in the Context folder when reviewing!

What was the outcome of the task enactment?

- What was learnt by doing the task?
- Was the task successful?
- Were there unexpected events or findings?
- If the task was repeated, what could be improved?
- Check what was found in the Context folder when reviewing!

Each mission will use tool-sheets to capture ideas, information and insights.
A mission has seven types of folders each with colour coded tool-sheets.

How to use mission tool-sheets

Tool-sheets to gather ideas, information and insights

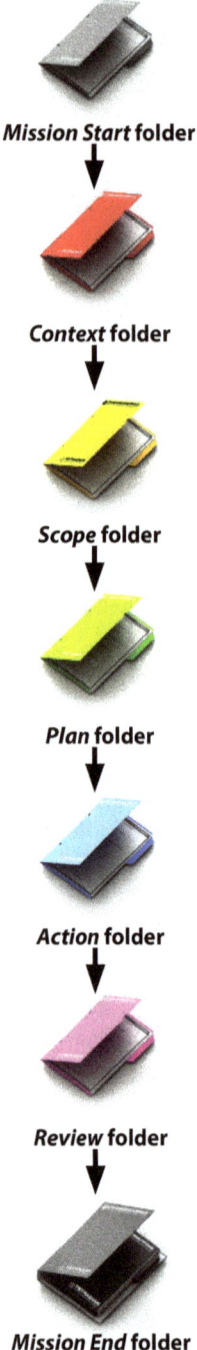

CHANGE→MAPPING
CONNECTING BUSINESS TOOLS TO MANAGE CHANGE

Mission Start **folder**

↓

Context **folder**

↓

Scope **folder**

↓

Plan **folder**

↓

Action **folder**

↓

Review **folder**

↓

Mission End **folder**

The cornerstone of any mission are the tool-sheets. They don't give solutions to problems. A pre-packaged solution might work for certain issues and fail miserably in others. Tool-sheets take a different approach by posing questions enabling a team to find the right answers. The basic tool-sheets pose generic questions allowing a team to fill in gaps about an issue. Rather than a pile of questions, the tool-sheets pose questions about a specific part of the issue. To help identify the tool-sheets they are colour-coded. Each tool-sheet will be associated with a certain folder within *Change-mapping*, as shown on the diagram on the left.

How to use the tool-sheets

General instructions

You will need to photocopy the blank tool-sheets when running missions to explore or resolve an issue.
See Part 2 for a selection of basic tool-sheets.

These tool-sheets are designed to be used by a small team of 4-12 **Explorers*** to capture ideas, information and insights during a mission. A **Pathfinder*** will make sure the Explorers stay on the task, while allowing unexpected insights to occur. An **Observer*** will note down all the team's findings on the tool-sheets and on additional paper if required.

Each tool-sheet has a general information section which is used to identify the issue, mission and the tool-sheet itself. It is strongly recommended to **not** skip certain folders as this can lead to errors when using *Change-mapping*, see **page 52** for more details.

Each section of the tool-sheet with circles asks the team to describe part of the issue. The circles are not meant to be answered in any order, but rather to start conversations. The questions in the circles are not meant to cover every possible question, but rather the team will add their own context specific questions to the generic questions. If you can't answer a question either skip it *(stating why)* or see **page 58** for advice about how to answer these questions.
See page 12 about the roles in Change-mapping.

Context basic tool-sheet 1 of 4 ⓘ CHANGE-MAPPING

General information

Mission identification:
Shimrin/0001/2.2.22/new exhibition stand enquiry
Sheet identification:
Shimrin/0001/2.2.22/new exhibition stand enquiry.context basic tool-sheet 1
The issue is:
Marketing manager believes we should invest in a new exhibition stand.
Our mission is:
To confirm to the board that we should invest in a new exhibition stand.

Describing the issue...

We have a new product and we need to promote it.

Our industry standard show is in Seattle in two months, many contacts will be there.

We need to make people aware of our new product, otherwise all that effort will be wasted.

We want an effective way to launch our product, is a stand was suggested.

- **Why does it happen?**
- **What happens?**
- **Where does it happen?**
- **Why does it need to be solved?**

- **Who is it happening to?** — Our organisation need an effective way to promote the new product.
- **When does it happen?** — The new product is ready to be launched now.
- **How does it happen?** — We are not sure if an exhibition stand is the best way to promote the new product.

How is the issue affected by...

- **Our organisation** — We think that we are sure if it is the most effective method.
- **Our clients** — Some of our clients visit trade shows but others prefer face to face meetings.
- **Our suppliers** — If our normal exhibition stand manufacturer is available to build a stand?
- **Our competitors** — Many of our competitors exhibit at the trade shows.

- **Time** — The exhibition is in two months.
- **Weather** — Delivering the exhibition might be tricky with spring floods.
- **Sustainability** — Can we reuse the stand for other shows?

- **Politics** — The unstable political climate makes any big investment risky.
- **Economics** — We have the change to the last minute which will raise the total price.
- **Social** — We need to be seen to be making a difference.
- **Technology** — Maybe a upgraded tech would be more effective?

- **Our industry** — We work in forest management which is facing huge change.
- **Information** — We should find out what our competitors are doing.
- **World events** — Our industry is hugely affected by increasing bush-fires.

Context basic tool-sheet 1 of 4 ⓘ CHANGE-MAPPING

General information

Mission identification:

Sheet identification:

The issue is:

Our mission is:

Describing the issue...

- **Why does it happen?**
- **What happens?**
- **Where does it happen?**
- **Why does it need to be solved?**

- **Who is it happening to?**
- **When does it happen?**
- **How does it happen?**

How is the issue affected by...

- **Our organisation**
- **Our clients**
- **Our suppliers**
- **Our competitors**

- **Time**
- **Weather**
- **Sustainability**

- **Politics**
- **Economics**
- **Social**
- **Technology**

- **Our industry**
- **Information**
- **World events**

Context basic tool-sheet 3 of 4 ⓘ CHANGE-MAPPING

General information

Mission identification:
Shimrin/0001/2.2.22/new exhibition stand enquiry
Sheet identification:
Shimrin/0001/2.2.22/new exhibition stand enquiry.context basic tool-sheet 3
The issue is:
Marketing manager believes we should invest in a new exhibition stand.
Our mission is:
To confirm to the board that we should invest in a new exhibition stand.

Which of these will take priority when the plan is being enacted?

INSIGHT
What do our clients respond to in terms of marketing?
We want to explore this further with a Scope Folder.

- **Security** — Keep our intellectual property protected.
- **Our clients** — Any solution communicates effectively with our clients.
- **Money** — Any last minute changes will lead to extra costs.

- **Our organisation** — Our brand and our employees are a priority.
- **Health & safety** — H and S must be priority number 1.
- **Sustainability** — Time pressure should not be at the expense of sustainability.

- **Short term** — Any solution should not leave us with long term problems.
- **Long term**
- **Value** — The solution should add value in that it effectively promotes our product.

- **Design**
- **Supply**
- **Weather** — We chose a stand then weather conditions would need to be managed.

- **Time** — Any solution needs to be done within two months or sooner.
- **Quality** — Our main priorities: health and safety and time.
- **This will be needed in the Action folder**

Context basic tool-sheet 3 of 4 ⓘ CHANGE-MAPPING

General information

Mission identification:

Sheet identification:

The issue is:

Our mission is:

Which of these will take priority when the plan is being enacted?

- **Security**
- **Our clients**
- **Money**

- **Our organisation**
- **Health & safety**
- **Sustainability**

- **Short term**
- **Long term**
- **Value**

- **Design**
- **Supply**
- **Weather**

- **Time**
- **Quality**
- **This will be needed in the Action folder**

Every tool-sheet page has a filled in version (blue text and arrows) to show you how to use it and a blank version which can be photocopied for your own missions.

Chapter 2: How to run a *Change-mapping* mission
Setting up a mission to explore or resolve an issue

In depth
This chapter has been designed for those unfamiliar with *Change-mapping* by illustrating a simple mission. But *Change-mapping* is not limited for use on small issues. Large scale issues such as those described in **Chapter 3** *(page 34)* also use the same method of breaking an unknown issue into smaller parts.
The main difference with larger issues is the amount of people involved and the flow of information.

In this chapter we explore how to run a basic *Change-mapping* mission.
To show how it works we will see how a *forestry management system manufacturer* might use *Change-mapping*.
In this example we can imagine that the marketing manager of the company wants to promote their new product. So to promote the new product she suggests investing in a new exhibition stand. Before exploring *how to invest* in a new stand, the organisation explores *if they should invest* in a new stand.
The next few pages show how this might work.

How to try Change-mapping
General instructions
Read through this chapter to see how a *Change-mapping* mission works for a simple issue.
Next gather a small team *(see page 12, to see who does what)* and follow each exercise in this chapter.
Each page has a simple exercise, shown with blue text, which uses the example of investing in a new stand *(see right)*.
After you have worked through this simple example, you should then be able to tackle different issues with *Change-mapping*.
The next stage might be to try *Change-mapping* on some of your organisations completed projects to see how it would work with them.
Then once you and your team are confident, then you could try it on small scale live issues before eventually moving to larger and more complex issues.
For more about larger scale *Change-mapping* missions see **chapters 3** and **12**.
Also page iii How to use this book.

The *Context* Folder
Setting the issue in context

In this folder we look at how the issue fits into the Big-picture. What is the Big-picture? In a mission we look at understanding the issue, how does it connect with the organisation's story and more. For example how is the issue affected by or affects: budgets, timings, logistics and so on.
To find out this information the Explorers will use the *Context* folder tool-sheets.
Other questions posed look at what laws and standards might affect a solution and what a successful outcome might look like.

30 minute exercise
'Shinrin needs a new exhibition stand!'

You will need to photocopy the blank Context Folder tool-sheets on pages 70, 72, 74 and 76.
Try to answer each part of the tool-sheets. When all the tool-sheet has been answered move to the next tool-sheet or folder (the *Scope* Folder).
If you can't answer a question either skip it (stating why) or see *Page 58* for advice about how to answer these questions.
When you have finished the folder then mark it with a green circle. This will show that this folder has been completed.
If later on in the mission something changes then change the circle back to red, showing that this folder is incomplete and needs to be revisited.

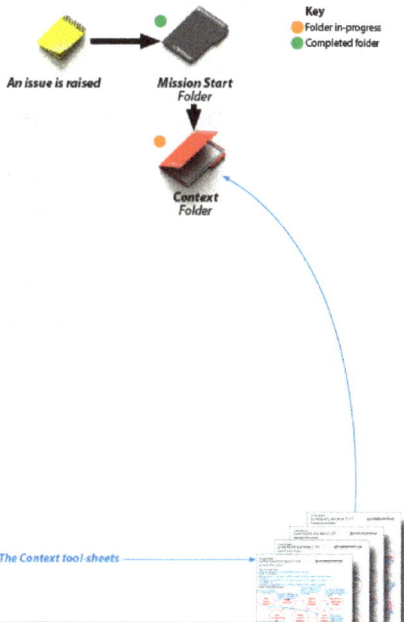

Key
🟠 Folder in-progress
🟢 Completed folder

An issue is raised — *Mission Start Folder*

Context Folder

The Context tool-sheets

The Context Folder
Here the team find out the context of the issue. Using tool-sheets questions are answered about the issue, what it is affecting/affected by and more.

The *Mission End* Folder
Reviewing the whole mission and what to do next

The *Mission End* folder works in the same way as the *Review* folders, except it reviews the *whole* mission. Using tool-sheets the team will review how everything went and if it stayed within the context for example. The other main thing this folder does is look at what happens *next*. Does the team want to treat the mission as a one-off or as part of a linked set of missions? A Linked mission is a mission which is connected to one or more missions, such as exploring if a new exhibition stand is required and then if so how to obtain the new exhibition stand *(see page 36 for an example of a Linked mission)*.

10 minute exercise
"We need a new exhibition stand!"

You will need to photocopy the blank Mission End Folder tool-sheet on page 98.
Try to answer each part of the tool-sheets. When all the tool-sheet has been answered mark the folder with a green circle. That is the end of the mission!
If you can't answer a question either skip it (stating why) or see *page 58* for advice about how to answer these questions.
All the information should be collected into one folder, so that it can be referred to in the future.

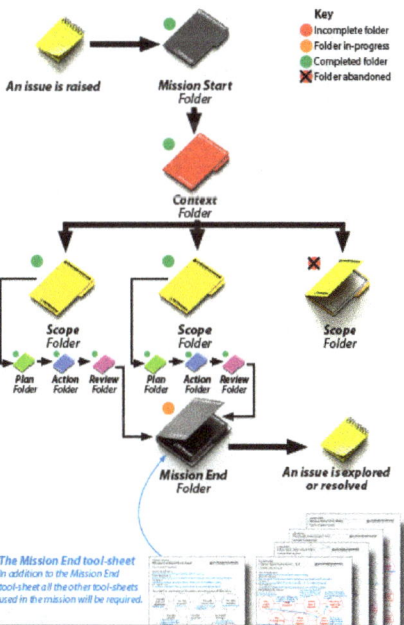

Key
🔴 Incomplete folder
🟠 Folder in-progress
🟢 Completed folder
❌ Folder abandoned

An issue is raised — *Mission Start Folder*

Context Folder

Scope Folder — *Scope Folder* — *Scope Folder*

Plan Folder Action Folder Review Folder   *Plan Folder Action Folder Review Folder*

Mission End Folder

An issue is explored or resolved

The Mission End tool-sheet
In addition to the Mission End tool-sheet all the other tool-sheets used in the mission will be required.

The Mission End Folder
Here the whole mission is reviewed. In the image above the Plan, Action and Review folders have been reduced in size. This way everything fits together neatly so that it is clear to understand.

In this chapter we show how a Change-mapping mission works step by step.

The *Mission Start* Folder

What is the mission trying to achieve?

In depth

The *Mission Start* folder works slightly differently to the other folders.

Before rushing to find out information, the *Mission Start* folder confirms what the issue to be resolved is. It acts in a similar way to a design brief by asking who is doing what.

Another key area is information sharing and storage. What if the information is needed by somebody else in six months?

If certain questions prove difficult to answer then the team can use a more detailed tool *(Page 112)* or Nested mission *(Page 114)* to answer the question.

Skipping questions.

Any question can be skipped but if they seem irrelevant, it might be worth examining why.

For example weather might seem unrelated to IT issues, unless computer systems were brought down by an electrical storm or flooding.

The *Mission Start* folder is used to set up missions, by using tool-sheets with a set of questions. The *Mission Start* folder asks what is the issue and what is the mission?

For example with the issue *"We need a new exhibition stand!"* the mission could be *" We will explore **why** we need a new exhibition stand. "* or *"We will explore **how to** get an exhibition stand".* This folder establishes what will actually happen in the mission, who will take part and what are the deliverables.

10 minute exercise

"We need a new exhibition stand!"

This exercise is a more detailed repeat of the simple mission shown at the end of the last chapter.

To run this part of the mission you will need a small team with 4-12 people who will be the **Explorers**.

Two more people will be the **Observer** and the **Pathfinder**. **You will need to photocopy the blank Mission Start Folder tool-sheets on pages 64 and 66.**

Try to answer each part of the tool-sheets. When all the tool-sheet has been answered move to the next tool-sheet or folder (the **Context** Folder).

If you can't answer a question either skip it *(stating why*, see left)* or see **Page 58** for advice about how to answer these questions.

When you have finished, mark the folder with a green circle.

An issue is raised

Mission Start
Folder

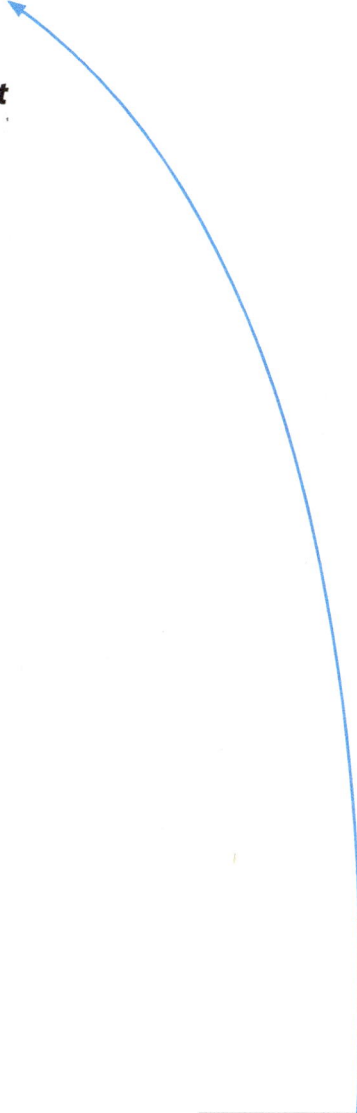

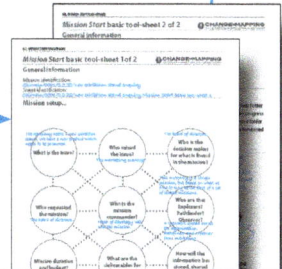

The Mission End tool-sheets

Mission Start basic tool-sheet 2 of 2
General information

Mission Start basic tool-sheet 1 of 2
General information

The Mission Start Folder

Here the mission to explore or resolve the issue is set up. Using tool-sheets the team works out questions such as who is involved, what is the mission is meant to do and more.

The *Context* Folder
Setting the issue in context

In depth
"The difference between reality and fiction? Fiction has to make sense."*

During a mission the Explorers should not expect answers straight away and feel free to admit that they don't know the answer to a question. Some of the questions may not seem relevant at first. They are designed to start conversations. Rather than a blank page the questions can help fill gaps in the context to help the team.

*https://en.wikiquote.org/wiki/ Tom_Clancy

In this folder we look at how the issue fits into the Big-picture. What is the Big-picture? In a mission we look at understanding the issue, how does it connect with the organisation's story and more. For example how is the issue affected by or affects: budgets, timings, logistics and so on.
To find out this information the Explorers will use the *Context* folder tool-sheets.
Other questions posed look at what laws and standards might affect a solution and what a successful outcome might look like.

30 minute exercise
"Shinrin needs a new exhibition stand!"

You will need to photocopy the blank Context Folder tool-sheets on pages 70,72, 74 and 76.
Try to answer each part of the tool-sheets. When all the tool-sheet has been answered move to the next tool-sheet or folder (the **Scope** Folder).
If you can't answer a question either skip it *(stating why)* or see **Page 58** for advice about how to answer these questions.
When you have finished the folder then mark it with a green circle. This will show that this folder has been completed.
If later on in the mission something changes then change the circle back to red, showing that the folder is incomplete and needs to be revisited.

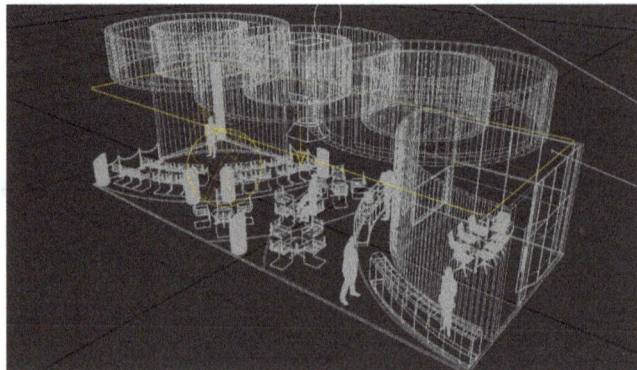

An issue is raised

Mission Start
Folder

Context
Folder

Key
- Folder in-progress
- Completed folder

The Context tool-sheets ———

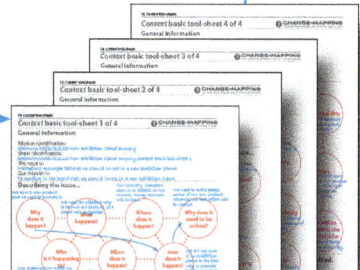

Context basic tool-sheet 1 of 4
Context basic tool-sheet 2 of 4
Context basic tool-sheet 3 of 4
Context basic tool-sheet 4 of 4

The Context Folder
Here the team find out the context of the issue. Using tool-sheets, questions are answered about the issue, what it is affecting/affected by and more.

The *Scope* Folder

Choosing options for what to do next to resolve the issue

In depth
Change-mapping acts as a map while exploring an unknown issue.
The *Context* Folder helps build a picture of how the issue fits into the context. The *Scope* Folders are used to decide what to do next to explore or resolve the issue, such as performing more research or constructing a final design.
In reality the team may want to explore multiple scopes of action.
This is easy to visualise with *Change-mapping*, with each scope having its own *Scope* folder. Each *Scope* folder is connected to the Pathway *(black arrows)* and has its own signalling system *(coloured circles)* so that the team can see which folders are completed.

At the end of the *Context* folder, the team can pick parts of the issue they want to explore further or resolve.
Each part has its own *Scope* folder. In our example *(right)* the team has three parts of the issue they want to explore or resolve further, so they will need three *Scope* folders.
Inside *Scope* folders the team will explore options they have to *explore* or *resolve* part of the issue.
Each option which they want to use will then have its own *Plan* folder, shown on the next page.

---

20 minute exercise
(for each Scope folder)
"Shinrin needs a new exhibition stand!"
You will need to photocopy the blank Scope Folder tool-sheets on pages 80 and 82.
Try to answer each part of the tool-sheets. When all the tool-sheet has been answered move to the next tool-sheet or folder (the **Plan** Folder).
If you can't answer a question either skip it *(stating why)* or see **Page 58** for advice about how to answer these questions.
Each *Scope* folder will have its own tool-sheets which need answering, as each *Scope* folder will be dealing with different parts of the issue.
When the folder has been completed then mark it with a green circle.

An issue is raised

Mission Start
Folder

Key
- Incomplete folder
- Folder in-progress
- Completed folder

Context
Folder

Scope
Folder

Scope
Folder

Scope
Folder

The Scope tool-sheets
In addition to the Scope
tool-sheets, Context tool-sheets
2 and 3 will be required.

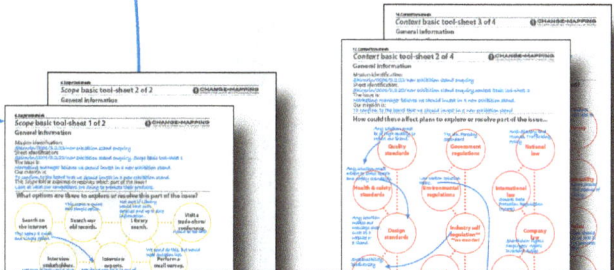

The Scope Folder
Each area to be explored or resolved (found in the Context folder) will have its own Scope folder.
In each folder options are explored to find to explore or resolve part of the issue.

The *Plan* Folder
Planning how to explore or resolve one part of the issue

In depth
"Fail to prepare, prepare to fail"*

If we go straight to the *Plan* Folder all kinds of problems can occur.

Are we planning to solve the wrong thing? Is the plan the best way to solve the issue? This is why we need the *Context* and *Scope* folders to help us avoid these errors.

"A plan is an assumption"

Any plan no matter how good is likely to be tested under real-world conditions. Can the plan cope with unexpected events? Do you have a back-up plan if the plan fails?

**https://en.wikiquote.org/wiki/
Benjamin_Franklin*

While the *Scope* folders were looking at multiple options in loose detail, the *Plan* folder looks at an individual project in greater detail. Here the team will plan how they will actually achieve the task. In the *Plan* folder they will look at what will be needed to set up the task, who will be involved, when it will take place and what to do if the unexpected occurs.

At the end the team should have a plan which allows part of the issue to be explored or resolved and is adaptable in case unexpected events occur.

---

30 minute exercise
(for each Plan folder)
"We need a new exhibition stand!"
You will need to photocopy the blank Plan Folder tool-sheets on pages 86 and 88.

Try to answer each part of the tool-sheets. When all the tool-sheet has been answered move to the next tool-sheet or folder (the **Action** Folder).

If you can't answer a question either skip it *(stating why)* or see **Page 58** for advice about how to answer these questions.

Each *Plan* folder will have its own tool-sheet which need answering, as each *Plan* folder will be dealing with different parts of the issue.

When the folder has been completed then mark it with a green circle.

An issue is raised

Mission Start
Folder

Context
Folder

Scope
Folder

Scope
Folder

Scope
Folder

Plan
Folder

The Plan tool-sheets
*In addition to the Plan
tool-sheets, Context tool-sheets
2 and 3 will be required and the
Scope tool-sheets.*

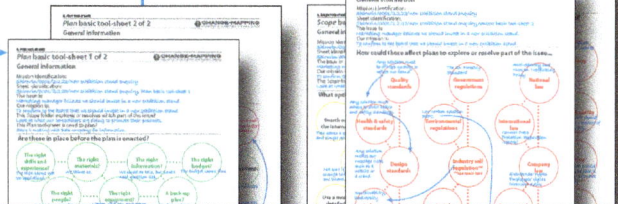

The Plan Folder
*Every Scope folder will have projects which need planning, this is done in the Plan folders.
Every project will have its own Plan folder, here just one Plan folder is shown for simplicity.*

The *Action* Folder

Exploring or resolving one part of the issue

In depth
The Action folders work slightly differently to the other folders.

You will do these tasks in the Action folder:
1. Pre-flight checklist before enacting the plan.
2. Enact the plan and perform the task, such as running an interview or building a prototype.
3. Collect any information which needed to be collected such as the interviewee's answers.
4. Record how the enactment of the plan was done. For example did the interviewer use leading questions or how was the prototype built.
This information will be required when in the *Review* folder.

The team used the *Plan* folder to produce a detailed plan of action. Now in its *Action* folder that plan is enacted. This folder is used as a pre-flight checklist, just before the action starts. It is also used to record the action taking place, this will be needed when the plan and action are reviewed. This will happen afterwards in the *Review* folder.

For example a team has planned to run an interview. In the *Action* folder they check everything is in place. They record the answers given by the *interviewee* and record how the *interviewer* ran the interview.

Timed exercise*
(For each Action folder)
"We need a new exhibition stand!"

You will need the **Plan folder tool-sheet 2** *(previously filled in by you, when you were in the Plan folder)* as a guide for when you are performing the action.
This will be used as a pre-flight checklist.
You will also need a **blank copy of Plan folder tool-sheet 2 (see page 26)** to record the enactment of the task. When the folder has been completed then mark it with a green circle.
*How long each Action folder takes will depend on what the actual action is, such as performing an interview compared to producing a prototype.

An issue is raised

Mission Start
Folder

Key

🔴 Incomplete folder
🟠 Folder in-progress
🟢 Completed folder

Context
Folder

Scope
Folder

Scope
Folder

Scope
Folder

Plan
Folder

Action
Folder

Required tool-sheets
A filled in Plan tool-sheet2,
a blank Plan tool-sheet2.

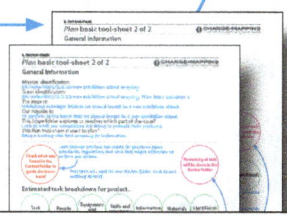

The Action Folder
Each Plan folder will plan how to explore or resolve part of the issue. The plan is enacted in its own
Action folder. No new tool-sheets are created in the Action folder as the plan is being enacted.

The *Review* Folder

Reviewing the exploration or resolution of one part of the issue

In depth
Its your fault!
The *Review* folder is not about blame finding. The US Army designed a system called the *After action review** to compare what was meant to happen with what actually happened, lessons learnt and what could be learnt from the difference. There will be risk in anything but sometimes inaction can be even worse. A more useful review will be where everyone works together to find where things went wrong, so that next time it should work better.
https://en.wikipedia.org/wiki/After-action_review

Once the team has performed one specific action in the mission, such as performing an interview, they will then use the *Review* folder. Here they compare how the action differed from what was planned to happen. Were there unexpected events and insights gained? If they were to repeat the process of performing an interview, what could be done better? Every *Action* folder will have its own *Review* folder. As with most of the other folders there are tool-sheets in the Review folder to help the team find out the information they need.

10 minute exercise
(for each Review folder)
"We need a new exhibition stand!"

You will need to photocopy the blank Review Folder tool-sheet on page 94.
Try to answer each part of the tool-sheet. When all the tool-sheet has been answered move to the next folder (the **Mission End** Folder).
If you can't answer a question either skip it *(stating why)* or see **Page 58** for advice about how to answer these questions.
Each *Review* folder will have its own tool-sheet which need answering, as each *Review* folder will be dealing with different parts of the issue.
When the folder has been completed then mark it with a green circle.

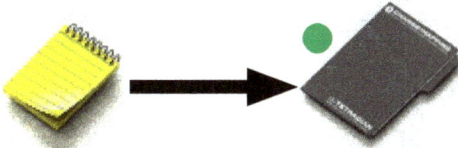

An issue is raised

🟢 *Mission Start* Folder

🟢 *Context* Folder

🟢 *Scope* Folder   🔴 *Scope* Folder   🔴 *Scope* Folder

🟢 *Plan* Folder   🟢 *Action* Folder   🟠 *Review* Folder

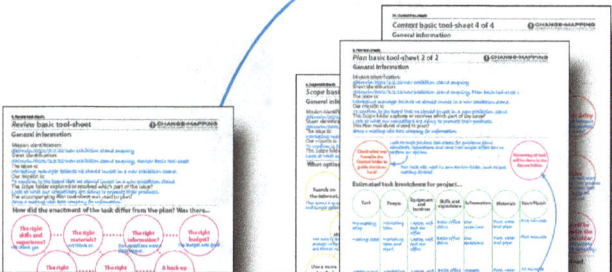

The Review tool-sheet
In addition to the Review tool-sheet a filled-in Plan tool-sheet 2 and Context tool-sheet 4 will be required. As well as the Scope tool-sheets.

The Review Folders
Every Plan and Action folder will have its own Review folder. Here the action is compared to the plan, what were the differences and what can be learnt.

The *Mission End* Folder
Reviewing the whole mission and what to do next

In depth
What happens next?
At this stage of a mission the team need to decide what to do next. For example if the team had been exploring if they need a new exhibition stand and the mission had confirmed that they do. Then the team could run a second Linked mission to see how to get a new exhibition stand. This second mission would work in the same way as the first, except that most of the context would most likely be the same as before.

Change-mapping is not limited to running small missions. It can be used for large scale missions with multiple teams and even multiple missions.

Chapter 03 *(Page 34)* shows how *Change-mapping* could be used to tackle complex issues such as the merging of three banks or the digital transformation of a city.

The *Mission End* folder works in the same way as the *Review* folders, except it reviews the **whole** mission. Using tool-sheets the team will review how everything went and if it stayed within the context for example. The other main thing this folder does is look at what happens **next**. Does the team want to treat the mission as a one-off or as part of a linked set of missions? A Linked mission is a mission which is connected to one or more missions, such as exploring if a new exhibition stand is required and then if so how to obtain the new exhibition stand *(see page 36 for an example of a Linked mission).*

10 minute exercise
"We need a new exhibition stand!"

You will need to photocopy the blank Mission End Folder tool-sheet on page 98.
Try to answer each part of the tool-sheet. When all the tool-sheet has been answered mark the folder with a green circle. That is the end of the mission!
If you can't answer a question either skip it *(stating why)* or see **page 58** for advice about how to answer these questions.
All the information should be collected into one folder, so that it can be referred to in the future.

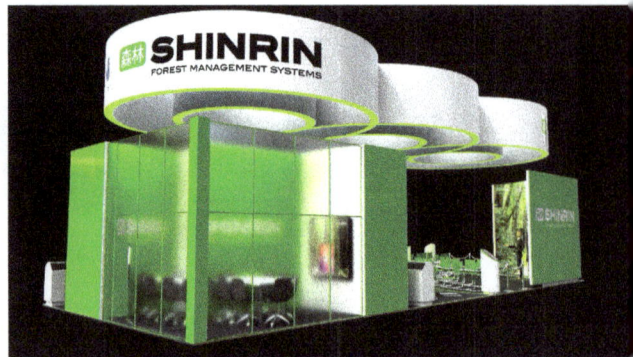

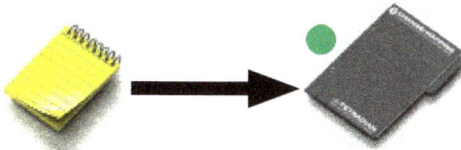

An issue is raised → **Mission Start** *Folder*

Key
- 🔴 Incomplete folder
- 🟠 Folder in-progress
- 🟢 Completed folder
- ❌ Folder abandoned

Context *Folder*

Scope *Folder*

Scope *Folder*

Scope *Folder*

Plan Folder **Action** Folder **Review** Folder

Plan Folder **Action** Folder **Review** Folder

Mission End *Folder*

An issue is explored or resolved

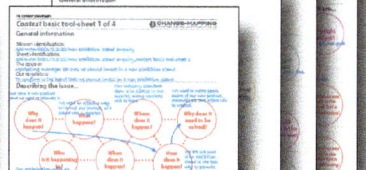

The Mission End tool-sheet
In addition to the Mission End tool-sheet all the other tool-sheets used in the mission will be required.

The Mission End Folder
Here the whole mission is reviewed. In the image above the Plan, Action and Review folders have been reduced in size. This way everything fits together neatly so that it is clear to understand.

Chapter 3: *Change-mapping* in action

Change-mapping in use with larger and more complex issues

In depth

The examples shown here are a brief introduction to larger and more complex missions to map issues affected by change.
These types of missions and others will be discussed in greater depth with detailed diagrams and tool-sheets in the companion book: **Advanced Change-mapping**.

In this chapter we show how *Change-mapping* can be used for more complex issues.

We continue the story of the company deciding if they should invest in a new exhibition stand and what happens next.

We also see *Change-mapping* being used for issues such as a bank merger, process integration and digital transformation.

These feature diagrams showing how *Change-mapping* works on these different issues.

The examples are loosely based on live projects which the author worked on as an enterprise architect across the world.

Specialised exercises

General instructions
In this chapter are a set of small exercises which tackle more detailed parts of *Change-mapping*. These are best done once you are familiar with missions, as they build on previous exercises shown in the book.

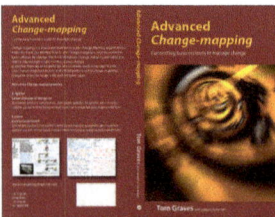

Regulation). This wide scale change in data sharing and storage can affect how an organisation functions. So one mission can be to understand what GDPR is, another can be to find out how it would affect the organisation. Another mission might be to see how the organisation would need to adapt based on what found in the previous missions. *https://en.wikipedia.org/wiki/General_Data_Protection_Regulation*

missions proceed.

10 minute exercise
'Information flow and storage'
This exercise looks at the kinds of issues posed by GDPR. Run one mission exploring what is GDPR.
Look at options for finding this information out, if you don't already. In a second mission a different team will look at how it will affect your organisation.
How will you share information between the two teams?
How often will you share that information?
How will you decide who can access that information?
How will you keep track of the information and make sure it is up to date?
Finding out the answers to these types of questions could be the focus of the second mission.

How to prepare for data regulation
Exploring how external factors can affect an organisation

Behind the story
This example is loosely based on how a wide scale change in legislation can affect an organisation. An example is GDPR *(General Data Protection Regulation)*. This wide scale change in data sharing and storage can affect how an organisation functions. So one mission can be to understand what GDPR is, another can be to find out how it would affect the organisation. Another mission might be to see how the organisation would need to adapt based on what found in the previous missions.
https://en.wikipedia. org/wiki/General_Data_ Protection_Regulation

In the example *(see left)* an organisation runs a mission to investigate new data regulations. This involves three *Scope* folders to obtain a wide range of information. Each *Scope* folder has its own team which shares information between each other. At the end of this mission they run a *Linked* mission to see how this will affect the organisation. A separate team run the second mission as information comes from the first rather than waiting for the first mission to end. A good information flow will be vital as both missions proceed.

10 minute exercise
'information flow and storage'
This exercise looks at the kinds of issues posed by GDPR. Run one mission exploring what is GDPR.
Look at options for finding this information out, if you don't already. In a second mission a different team will look at how it will affect your organisation.
How will you share information between the two teams?
How often will you share that information?
How will you decide who can access that information?
How will you keep track of the information and make sure it is up to date?
Finding out the answers to these types of questions could be the focus of the second mission.

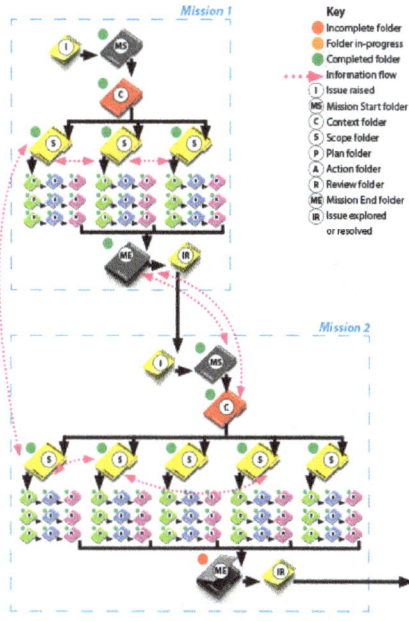

Mission 1

Key
- Incomplete folder
- Folder in-progress
- Completed folder
- Information flow
- (I) Issue raised
- (MS) Mission Start folder
- (C) Context folder
- (S) Scope folder
- (P) Plan folder
- (A) Action folder
- (R) Review folder
- (ME) Mission End folder
- (IR) Issue explored or resolved

Mission 2

An example of two missions linked with a common issue
In this example a team finds out about data legislation and then how it will affect the organisation. Following missions (not shown) will look at what the organisation will need to change.

How to use digital transformation
Connecting different organisations across a city

Behind the story
This example of how Change-mapping could be used is loosely based on an actual fishing town in Southern Europe which faces problems with falling tourism and fishing. The author met two designers who wanted to use digital solutions to connect organisations across the town to benefit all in the space.

The digital transformation of a city would be a massive mission made up of many interconnected smaller missions. *Change-mapping* could be used to explore how it might benefit a city and its inhabitants. Most probably such a large scale mission would start by setting digital transformation in the context of the city. For example using the *'internet of things'** to make the city's tram network *'reactive'*, allowing it to react to increased demand when and where it was needed rather than having a huge fleet of trams. Once the exploration of digital transformation proved it would benefit the city, then linked parallel missions would be undertaken. These would look at implementing and maintaining such systems, so that the vision of the digital transformation was achieved.
**https://en.wikipedia.org/wiki/Internet_of_things*

60 minute exercise
'Digital transformation of an organisation'
Run a simple mission looking at how digital transformation** might affect your organisation. What would be the context for digital transformation inside your organisation? How might it affect your organisation and what it does?
**https://en.wikipedia.org/wiki/Digital_transformation*

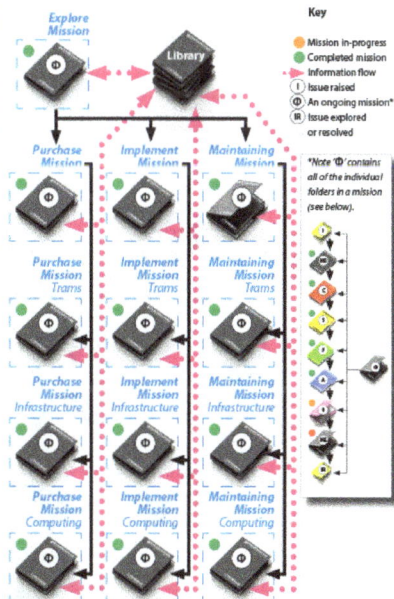

Explore Mission

Library

Key
- Mission in-progress
- Completed mission
- Information flow
- (I) Issue raised
- (D) An ongoing mission*
- Issue explored or resolved

*Note 'D' contains all of the individual folders in a mission (see below).

Purchase Mission / Implement Mission / Maintaining Mission

Purchase Mission Trams / Implement Mission Trams / Maintaining Mission Trams

Purchase Mission Infrastructure / Implement Mission Infrastructure / Maintaining Mission Infrastructure

Purchase Mission Computing / Implement Mission Computing / Maintaining Mission Computing

An example of missions to digitally transform a city
A very large scale and highly complex set of missions have been broken down into connected parts which share information and their current progress with each other.

This chapter shows Change-mapping in action.

How to invest in a new exhibition stand

Finding out *how* to invest, after finding out *if* to invest

Behind the story

This example of how *Change mapping* could be used is loosely based on a project that the author was involved with.

A healthcare product manufacturer was considering how to invest in a new training centre to promote its products. The author worked with the manufacturer to establish that a training area matched the context of the issue. Once this was established *Change-mapping* was used to start mapping out how to design and build a new training centre.

This is an example of a Linked mission. A linked mission is linked to one or more missions by the same issue. In the example *(right)* an issue is raised that a company needs a new exhibition stand. This issue had a mission to *find out if* the company required a new stand. At the end of the mission it was found that the company should invest in a new stand. So then a second *(Linked)* mission was started to *find out how* to invest in a new stand. The second mission works in the same way as the first, except that most of the context information can be drawn straight from the first mission.

10 minute exercise

"We need to have a dedicated seating area on our stand"
This exercise looks at questioning an issue. Rather than just looking at how to get a dedicated seating area, look at possible alternatives.
Who might have decided that a seating area is required and what might they have based their view on?
Would your team feel free to challenge the view about the seating area if they could think of an alternate idea?
The point of the exercise is to establish the logic behind an issue and to challenge it if required.

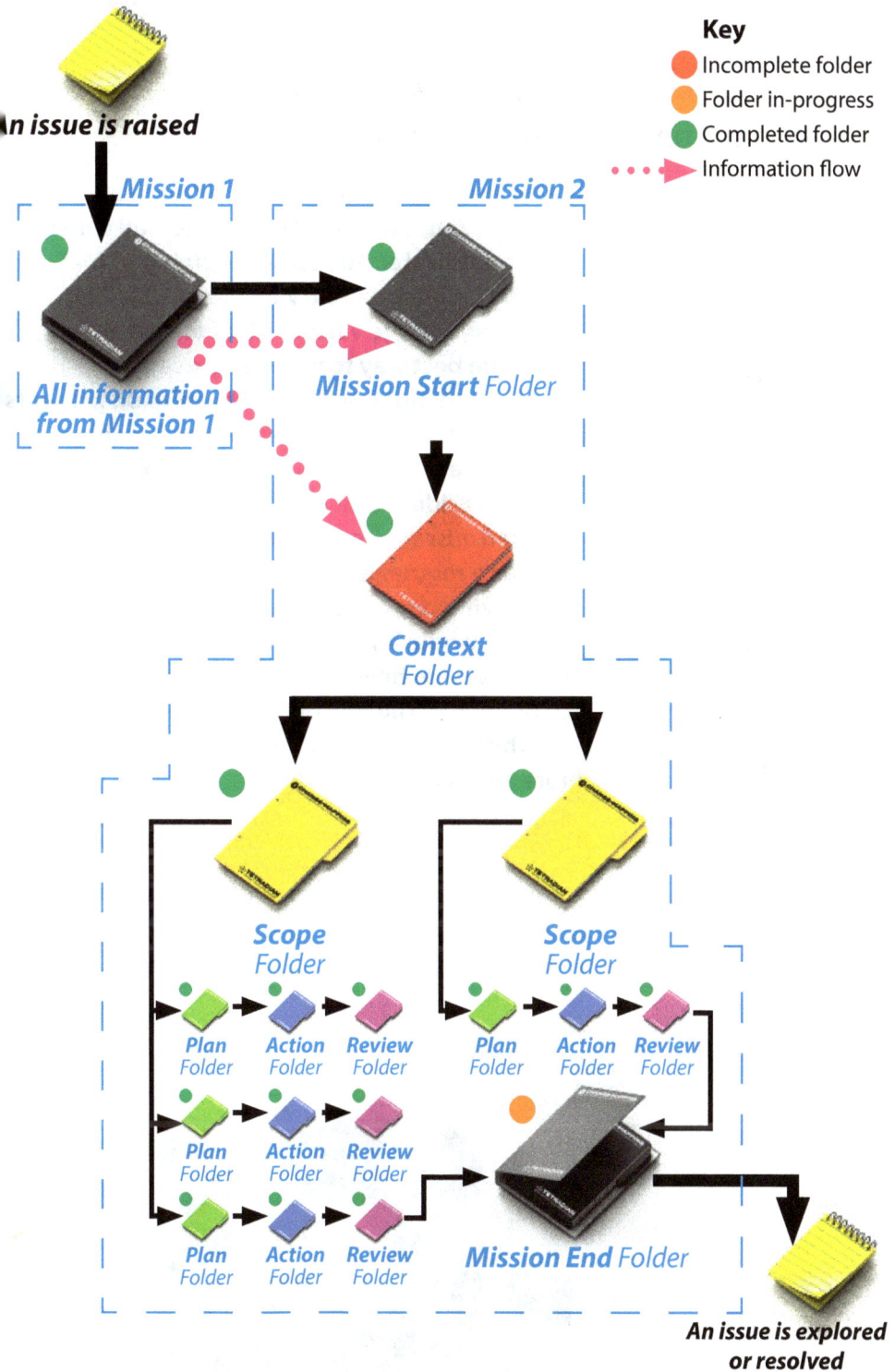

Key
- Incomplete folder
- Folder in-progress
- Completed folder
- ··········► Information flow

An issue is raised

Mission 1

Mission 2

Mission Start Folder

All information from Mission 1

Context Folder

Scope Folder

Scope Folder

Plan Folder   *Action* Folder   *Review* Folder

Plan Folder   *Action* Folder   *Review* Folder

Plan Folder   *Action* Folder   *Review* Folder

Plan Folder   *Action* Folder   *Review* Folder

Mission End Folder

An issue is explored or resolved

An example of a Linked mission
*In this example one mission found out **if** a new exhibition stand was required, while the second mission found out **how** to invest in a new exhibition stand.*

How to find out why a product is failing

Changing the unknown to the known

Behind the story

This example of how *Change mapping* could be used is loosely based on a project that the author was involved with.

A healthcare product manufacturer had found that its packaging was failing somewhere in the supply chain. The manufacturer had to establish if the issue was a result of the external logistics company, a design issue or some other factor.

In this example a watch manufacturer has received complaints that its watches fail when used in salt water. The team are trying to find out *why* it is failing before trying to *stop it* failing. At the *Scope* stage various ideas are discussed about the best way to find out the cause of the problem. But one part of the mission presents a question that they can't answer using the basic questions and even with a dedicated tool-sheet. So they decide to use a *Nested* mission.

A *Nested mission (see right)* works exactly the same as a regular mission, except that is exploring or resolving **one question** about the issue, rather than the whole issue.

Once the team finish the *Nested mission* they continue with the rest of the main mission to find out why the watch is failing. See page 114 for more about *Nested missions*.

10 minute exercise

"Why is our watch failing?"

How might you tackle finding out why a watch is failing in salt-water? How would you break down the task into parts? How would you avoid bias in your mission, for example not assuming salt-water was the problem until the evidence confirmed it was?

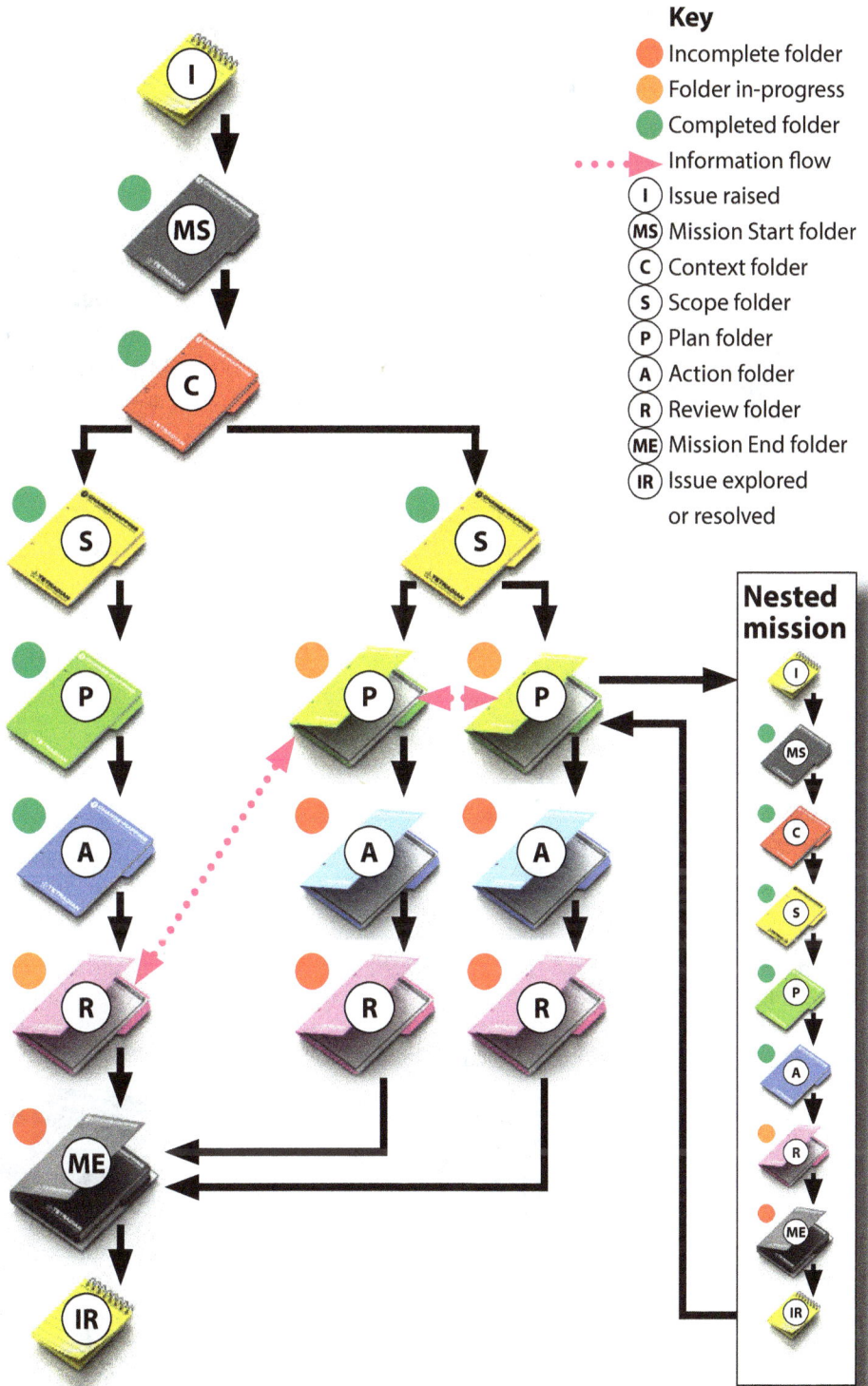

Key

- 🔴 Incomplete folder
- 🟠 Folder in-progress
- 🟢 Completed folder
- ▪▪▪▪▶ Information flow
- (I) Issue raised
- (MS) Mission Start folder
- (C) Context folder
- (S) Scope folder
- (P) Plan folder
- (A) Action folder
- (R) Review folder
- (ME) Mission End folder
- (IR) Issue explored or resolved

Nested mission

An example of a mission with a Nested mission

In this example during a mission the team have not been able to answer a question, even with a more detailed pre-selected tool. So they use a Nested mission to answer the question.

How to prepare for data regulation

Exploring how external factors can affect an organisation

Behind the story

This example is loosely based on how a wide scale change in legislation can affect an organisation. An example is GDPR *(General Data Protection Regulation)**. This wide scale change in data sharing and storage can affect how an organisation functions.

So one mission can be to understand what GDPR is, another can be to find out how it would affect the organisation. Another mission might be to see how the organisation would need to adapt based on what found in the previous missions.

*https://en.wikipedia.org/wiki/ General_Data_Protection_Regulation

In the example *(see left)* an organisation runs a mission to investigate new data regulations. This involves three *Scope* folders to obtain a wide range of information. Each *Scope* folder has its own team which shares information between each other. At the end of this mission they run a *Linked mission* to see how this will affect the organisation. A separate team run the second mission as information comes from the first rather than waiting for the first mission to end. A good information flow will be vital as both missions proceed.

10 minute exercise

"Information flow and storage"

This exercise looks at the kinds of issues posed by GDPR.
Run one mission exploring what is GDPR.
Look at options for finding this information out.
In a second mission a different team will look at how it will affect your organisation.
How will you share information between the two teams?
How often will you share that information?
How will you decide who can access that information?
How will you keep track of the information and make sure it is up to date?
Finding out the answers to these types of questions could be the focus of the second mission.

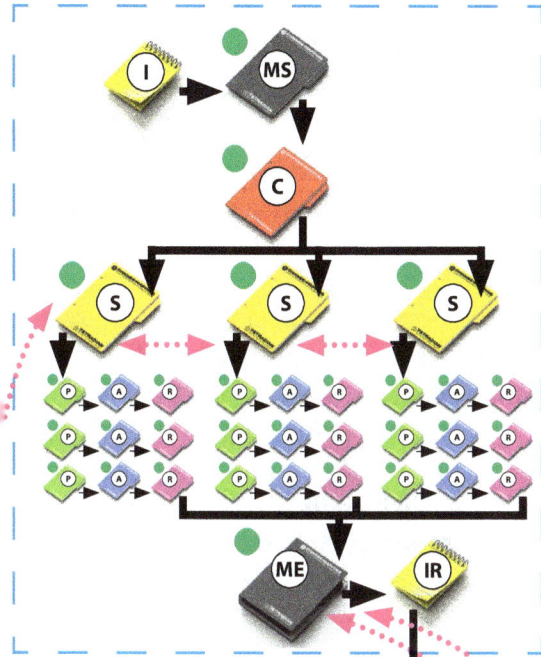

Key

🔴 Incomplete folder
🟠 Folder in-progress
🟢 Completed folder
•••••➤ Information flow
(I) Issue raised
(MS) Mission Start folder
(C) Context folder
(S) Scope folder
(P) Plan folder
(A) Action folder
(R) Review folder
(ME) Mission End folder
(IR) Issue explored
  or resolved

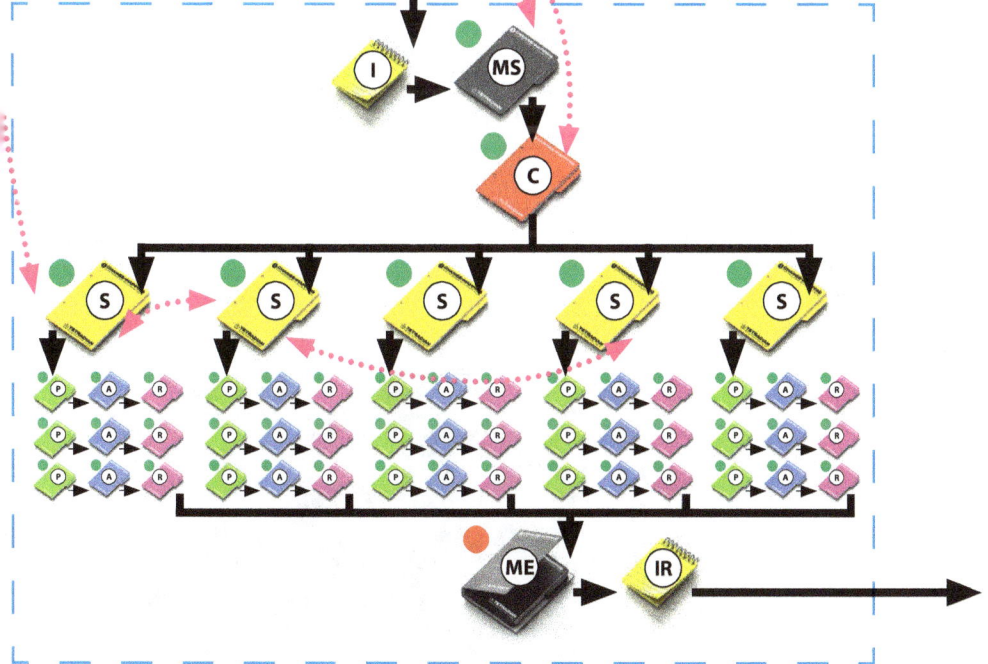

An example of two missions linked with a common issue

In this example a team finds out about data legislation and then how it will affect the organisation. Following missions (not shown) will look at what the organisation will need to change.

How to rationalise a logistics infrastructure

Making sure everyone works together at the right time

Behind the story
This example of how *Change mapping* could be used is loosely based on how oranges are brought from the farmers to the supermarket. Often we take items in the supermarket for granted. But the massive logistics effort of growing crops in one country, transporting them over an ocean and having them fresh in store is worth examining. No one part of the chain is more important than the other. It can be interesting looking at how all the items in the supermarket are mostly the result of highly complex logistics efforts.

This example looks at the complicated logistics involved in getting perishable oranges from one country to another on time and to the highest quality. Using *Change-mapping* we can break down this enormous task into smaller missions. Simplifying it into three main parallel missions which themselves are linked. As well they will use an OODA loop *(see page 44)* to repeat the process throughout the year. Information flow with such a complex issue will be critical to help react to unpredictable issues, such as the weather.

30 minute exercise
"Who is more important!"
This exercise asks a team to look at the different parts of a logistics chain to ask 'Who is more important?'
Assemble 6-8 people around a table. Each person will represent one part of the orange growing, transporting and retailing chain. They will describe how important their part of the chain is and how other parts of the chain could be improved.
Now once all have spoken, all move round one place at the table and have each person state the case for where they are now. The idea is often people become entrenched in one department and feel isolated from other departments. By sitting in others' shoes people often see that they wouldn't do things differently.

Key

- 🟠 Mission in-progress
- 🟢 Completed mission
- ●●▶ Information flow
- Ⓘ Issue raised
- Ⓟ An ongoing mission*
- ⒾⓇ Issue explored or resolved

*Note 'Φ' contains all of the individual folders in a mission (see below).

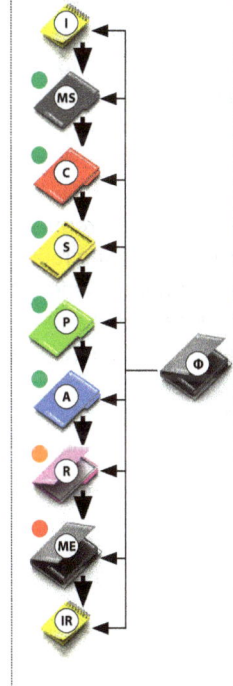

Sow crops Mission

Pack Mission

Tend crops Mission

Harvest crops Mission

Transport Mission

Coordinate Mission

Unload Mission

Marketing Mission

Sell Mission

Library

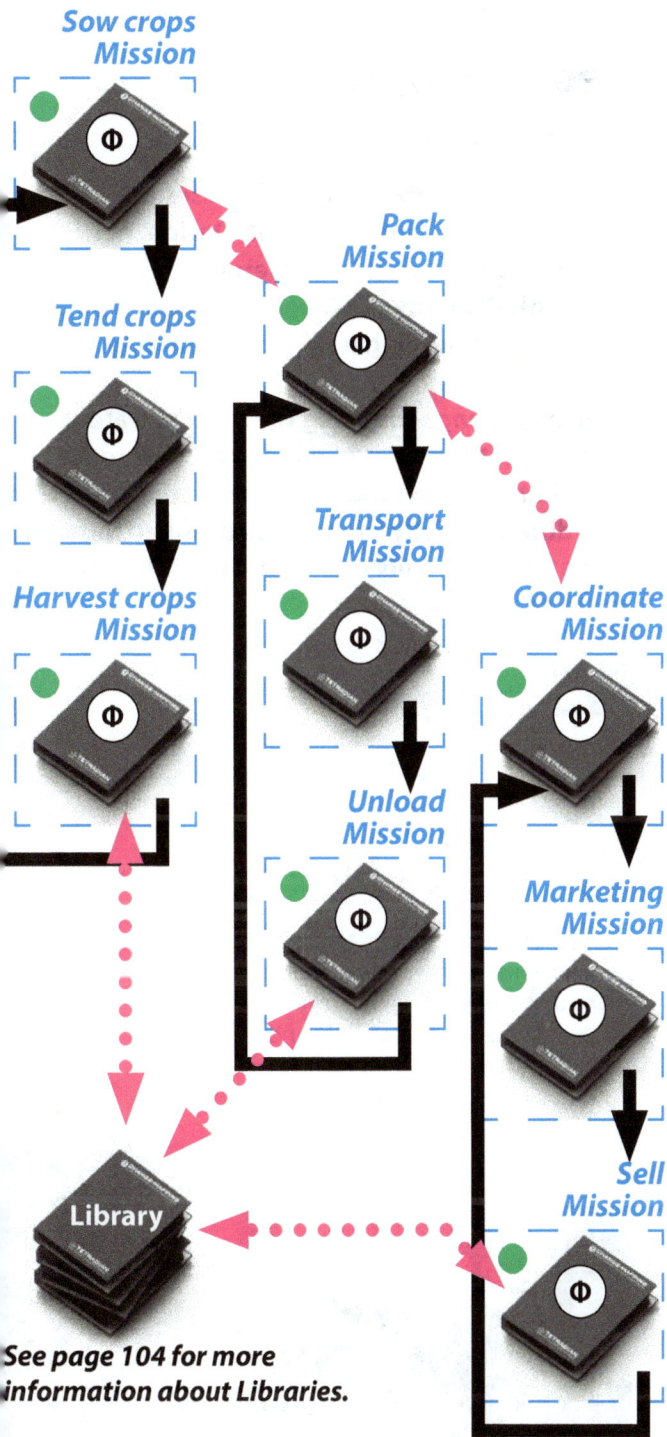

See page 104 for more information about Libraries.

An example of missions used in a large infrastructure issue
A simplified example of a massively complex logistics challenge.

How to merge three corporate banks

Making sure that change benefits all

Behind the story
This example of how *Change mapping* could be used is loosely based on a project that the author was involved with.
A large multi-national bank with branches spread across the country had recently merged. The board was tasked with finding out why the banks reputation was plummeting rapidly. The author working with a local team built a detailed picture of the difference between what the staff and board felt was actually happening.

The example shown on the right uses an OODA loop* which is Observe, Orient, Decide, Act. Recently three banks have merged.
Although the banks CEO believes the bank is doing well, troubling news from front line staff tells a different story.
So using *Change-mapping* the bank's strategy department run a set of linked missions to find out what is happening and do something about it. This differs slightly from a typical linked mission in that it continually monitors what is happening to stop problems reoccurring.
*https://en.wikipedia.org/wiki/OODA_loop

60 minute exercise
"OODA loop"
Imagine that you were the strategy department of the bank.
How might you use an OODA loop to **Observe** what was happening across the whole bank?
How would you **Orient** where the bank is, with where they should be?
How would you **Decide** how to best bring about that change?
How would you **Act** to bring about that change?
Each stage would require its own mission looking at the context, scopes of action, plans and so on.
With the OODA loop there would be a continuous loop to see how those changes have affected the bank.

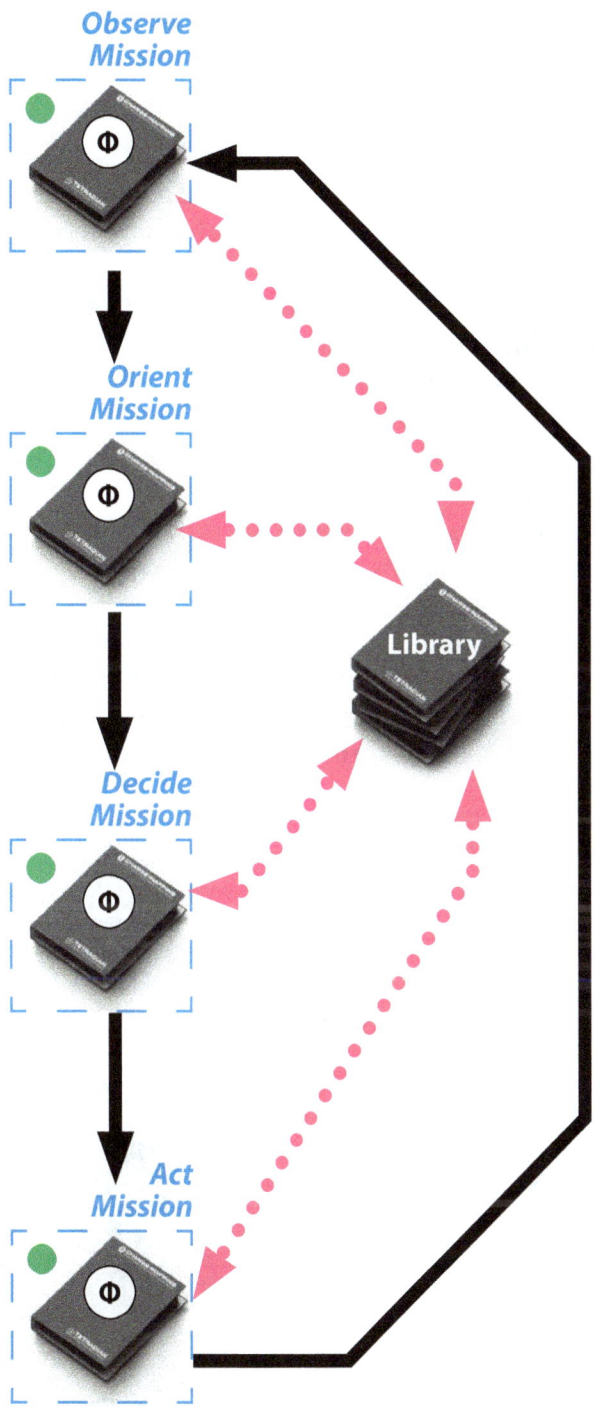

Key

- 🟠 Mission in-progress
- 🟢 Completed mission
- ⦙⦙▶ Information flow
- (I) Issue raised
- (Φ) An ongoing mission*
- (IR) Issue explored or resolved

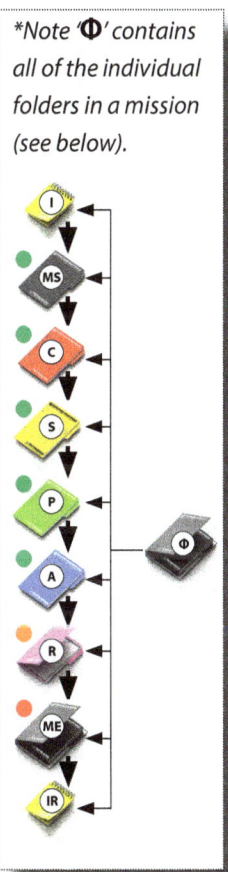

*Note 'Φ' contains all of the individual folders in a mission (see below).

An example of missions to bring change to a struggling multi-national bank

A set of missions using the OODA loop (see main text) to find out what is going wrong with the bank and to then bring about structured change.

How to scale up production
Taking things to the next level

Behind the story

This example of how *Change mapping* could be used is loosely based on a small drinks manufacturer who had produced a new type of fruit drink.

They wanted to increase sales by selling the drink to a major supermarket. The leap from small scale sales, packaging and logistics proved challenging.

The supermarket had a wide range of requirements the drinks manufacturer would have to satisfy before them agreeing to sell the fruit drink.

A large amount of risk, including investment in new packaging and production facilities meant that the future needed to be made as clear as possible before the drinks manufacturer decided what to do next.

A small organisation has developed a new drone. They have recently received massive orders far beyond their current capabilities.

So they decide to use *Change-mapping* to explore and ultimately resolve the unknowns with scaling-up production.

They run parallel missions *(Mission 1 on diagram)* exploring finance, manufacturing, logistics and more.

Then with this information they run linked missions *(Mission 2 on diagram)* looking at running scenarios imagining they had increased production, to test for faults before they happen. The last linked missions *(Mission 3 on diagram)* look at bringing all this information to prepare them to actually start increased production

10 minute exercise
"Scale up"

This exercise is to run a simple mission looking in brief at how would you cope with a 500% increase in demand for your product or services. Use the mission to explore how you would ramp up production. What legislation for example might come into play when you scale up production?

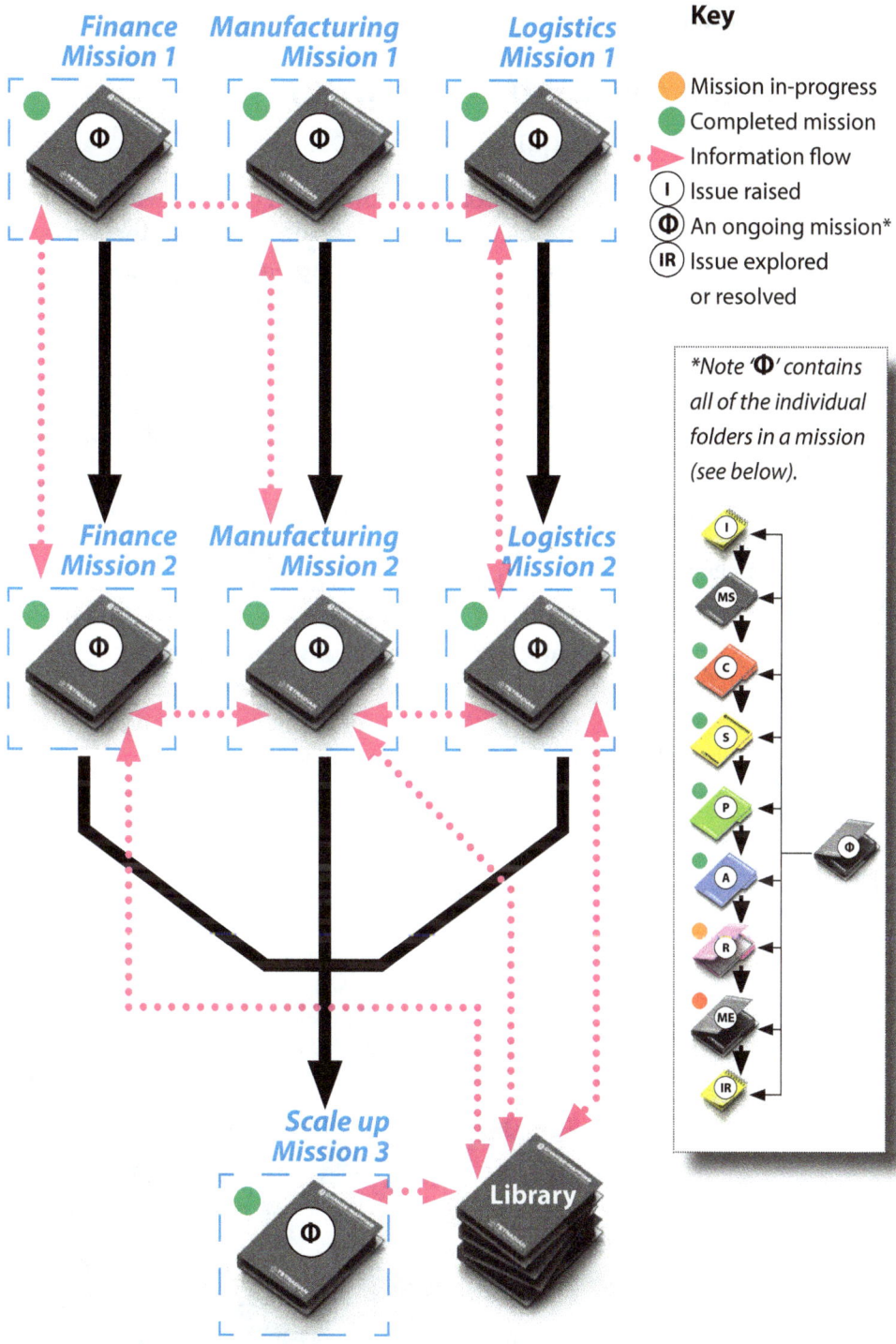

Key

- 🟠 Mission in-progress
- 🟢 Completed mission
- ···▶ Information flow
- Ⓘ Issue raised
- Φ An ongoing mission*
- ⓘR Issue explored or resolved

*Note 'Φ' contains all of the individual folders in a mission (see below).

Finance Mission 1

Manufacturing Mission 1

Logistics Mission 1

Finance Mission 2

Manufacturing Mission 2

Logistics Mission 2

Scale up Mission 3

Library

An example of parallel missions to bring explore scaling up a business

A set of parallel missions investigate parts of the issue. Each of these are taken further with linked missions and a final combined mission.

How to use digital transformation
Connecting different organisations across a city

Behind the story
This example of how *Change mapping* could be used is loosely based on an actual fishing town in Southern Europe which faces problems with falling tourism and fishing.
The author met two designers who wanted to use digital solutions to connect organisations across the town to benefit all in the space.

The digital transformation of a city would be a massive mission made up of many interconnected smaller missions. *Change-mapping* could be used to explore how it might benefit a city and its inhabitants. Most probably such a large scale mission would start by setting digital transformation in the context of the city. For example using the '*Internet of things*'* to make the city's tram network '*reactive*', allowing it to react to increased demand when and where it was needed rather than having a huge fleet of trams. Once the exploration of digital transformation proved it would benefit the city, then linked parallel missions would be undertaken. These would look at implementing and maintaining such systems, so that the vision of the digital transformation was achieved.
*https://en.wikipedia.org/wiki/Internet_of_things

60 minute exercise
"Digital transformation of an organisation"
Run a simple mission looking at how digital transformation** might affect your organisation. What would be the context for digital transformation inside your organisation? How might it affect your organisation and what it does?
**https://en.wikipedia.org/wiki/Digital_transformation

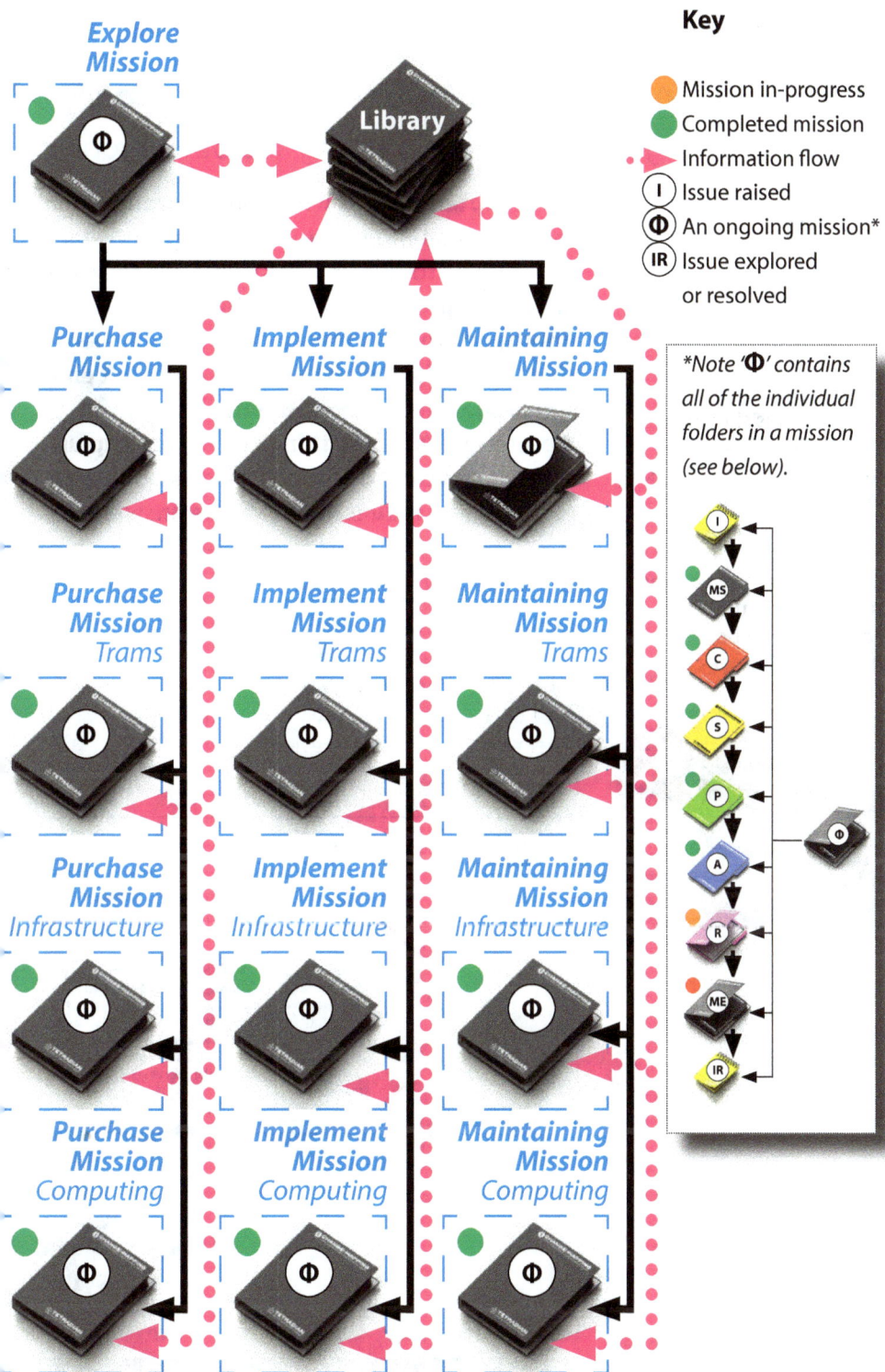

An example of missions to digitally transform a city

A very large scale and highly complex set of missions have been broken down into connected parts which share information and their current progress with each other.

Chapter 4: *Common problems with Change-mapping*
Avoiding rushing to solve the wrong thing and other problems

In depth
The problems shown in this chapter are some of the most common things which can affect *Change-mapping* missions.
More about how to tackle these and other problems is discussed in the accompanying book:
Advanced Change-mapping

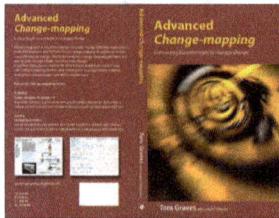

This chapter looks at what can go wrong when using *Change-mapping*. One example is when people *miss* folders in a mission, which can lead to enormous problems later on in the mission. Another problem shown is when people become *stuck* in one folder, so that a mission can't end which again leads to problems.
We also look at some things which can trip up a mission such as deciding the level of detail required and if questions can't be answered.

Specialised exercises
General instructions
In this chapter are a set of small exercises which tackle common problems with *Change-mapping*. These are best done once you are familiar with missions, as they connect to other exercises shown in previous chapters.

by Pauline Grant MA
https://en.wikipedia.org/wiki/Strategy

10 minute exercise
"It's obvious!"
Take one member of the team who is very skilled and familiar with something such as drawing.
Now get them to explain it to another member of the team who is unfamiliar with how to draw.
What happens when the expert explains things which are obvious to them but not to the second person?
This can be a silent enemy of solving issues of change.
If somebody knows they don't know something then they most likely will accept assistance. But much trickier is when someone thinks they know when in fact they don't.
This can lead to enormous problems as the person genuinely believes they are following the right direction when in fact they are not.

EDINBURGH AIRPORT 7/7/9

Jumping to the wrong part of a mission

Jumping straight to a plan, rushing to action and more

Further reading
HBR's 10 Must Reads
on Strategy
by Harvard Business
Review, Michael E. Porter,
et al.
Business Psychology in
Practice
by Pauline Grant MA
https://en.wikipedia.org/
wiki/Strategy

These types of problems can occur when panic sets in. An issue is raised and people rush to start planning how to resolve the issue. At first glance it might not seem like a problem, but it misses important parts. Why does the issue need solving? Is the chosen method to solve it the best one? Another similar problem can be when people rush into action without even having a plan.
These types of problem can be countered by assessing the issue and then when it is understood a better solution is likely to present itself.

10 minute exercise

"It's obvious!"
Take one member of the team who is very skilled and familiar with something such as drawing.
Now get them to explain it to another member of the team who is unfamiliar with how to draw.
What happens when the expert explains things which are obvious to them but not to the second person?
This can be a silent enemy of solving issues of change. If somebody knows they don't know something then they most likely will accept assistance. But much trickier is when someone thinks they know when in fact they don't.
This can lead to enormous problems as the person genuinely believes they are following the right direction when in fact they are not.

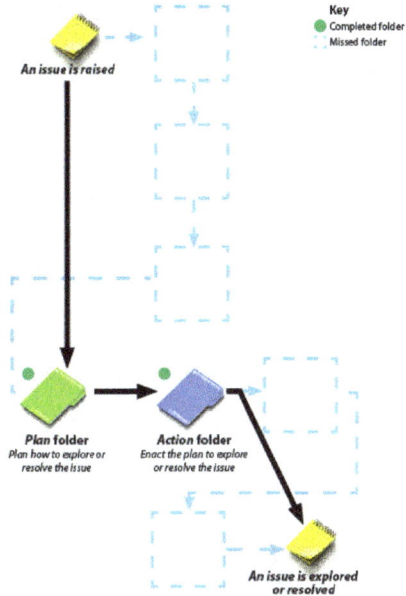

Key
- ● Completed folder
- ⬜ Missed folder

An issue is raised

Plan folder
Plan how to explore or
resolve the issue

Action folder
Enact the plan to explore
or resolve the issue

**An issue is explored
or resolved**

Rushing straight to the plan
While this approach may work, it misses important steps, such as asking
"Why does the issue need resolving".

Staying stuck in one part of a mission

Analysis paralysis, office politics and more

Further reading
Thinking, Fast and Slow
by Daniel Kahneman
Crucial Conversations Tools
for Talking When Stakes
Are High
by Kerry Patterson
Corporate Strategy:
Tools for Analysis
and Decision-Making
by Phanish Puranam

This problem is the opposite of rushing into one part of a mission. Here a team will progress through a mission and then grind to a halt.
Most of these issues such as analysis paralysis and office politics can be traced to decision making. With analysis paralysis a team believes they need to do just one more bit of analysis, with the result that nothing actually is changed. And with office politics people will argue over favoured approaches but often the issue still stays unresolved.
These types of problems can be countered by strong unbiased leadership and firm decision making using all available information.

10 minute exercise

"We can't decide!"
In this simple exercise a small team imagine they are on a tiny island which may soon be swamped by the ocean. They can stay where they are, where there is food and water or they can try to swim for a nearby island which is not flooding but may not have food and water.
They can't bring the food and water with them.
What should they do? The exercise looks in brief about making decisions with limited information and time.

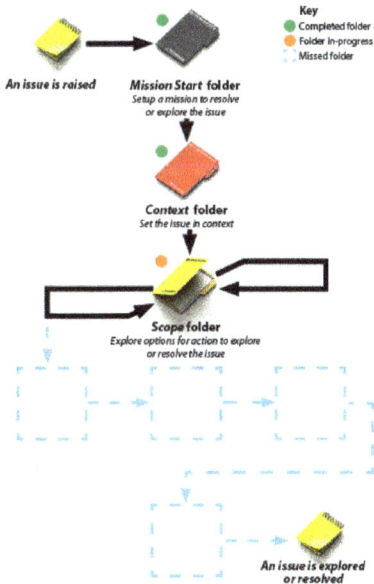

Key
- ● Completed folder
- ● Folder in-progress
- ⬜ Missed folder

An issue is raised

Mission Start folder
Setup a mission to resolve
or explore the issue

Context folder
Set the issue in context

Scope folder
Explore options for action to explore
or resolve the issue

**An issue is explored
or resolved**

Staying stuck in one part of a mission
Here a mission reaches the Scope folder and then grinds to a halt.
Until this is resolved the mission can't be completed.

This chapter highlights common mistakes when using Change-mapping.

Jumping to the wrong part of a mission

Jumping straight to a plan, rushing to action and more

Further reading
HBR's 10 Must Reads
on Strategy
by Harvard Business
Review, Michael E. Porter,
et al.
*Business Psychology in
Practice*
by Pauline Grant MA
https://en.wikipedia.org/
wiki/Strategy

These types of problems can occur when panic sets in. An issue is raised and people rush to start planning how to resolve the issue. At first glance it might not seem like a problem, but it misses important parts. Why does the issue need solving? Is the chosen method to solve it the best one? Another similar problem can be when people rush into action without even having a plan.

These types of problem can be countered by assessing the issue and then when it is understood a better solution is likely to present itself.

10 minute exercise

"It's obvious!"

Take one member of the team who is very skilled and familiar with something such as drawing.

Now get them to explain it to another member of the team who is unfamiliar with how to draw.

What happens when the expert explains things which are obvious to them but not to the second person?

This can be a silent enemy of solving issues of change.

If somebody knows they don't know something then they most likely will accept assistance. But much trickier is when someone thinks they know when in fact they don't.

This can lead to enormous problems as the person genuinely believes they are following the right direction when in fact they are not.

EDINBURGH AIRPORT 7/7/19

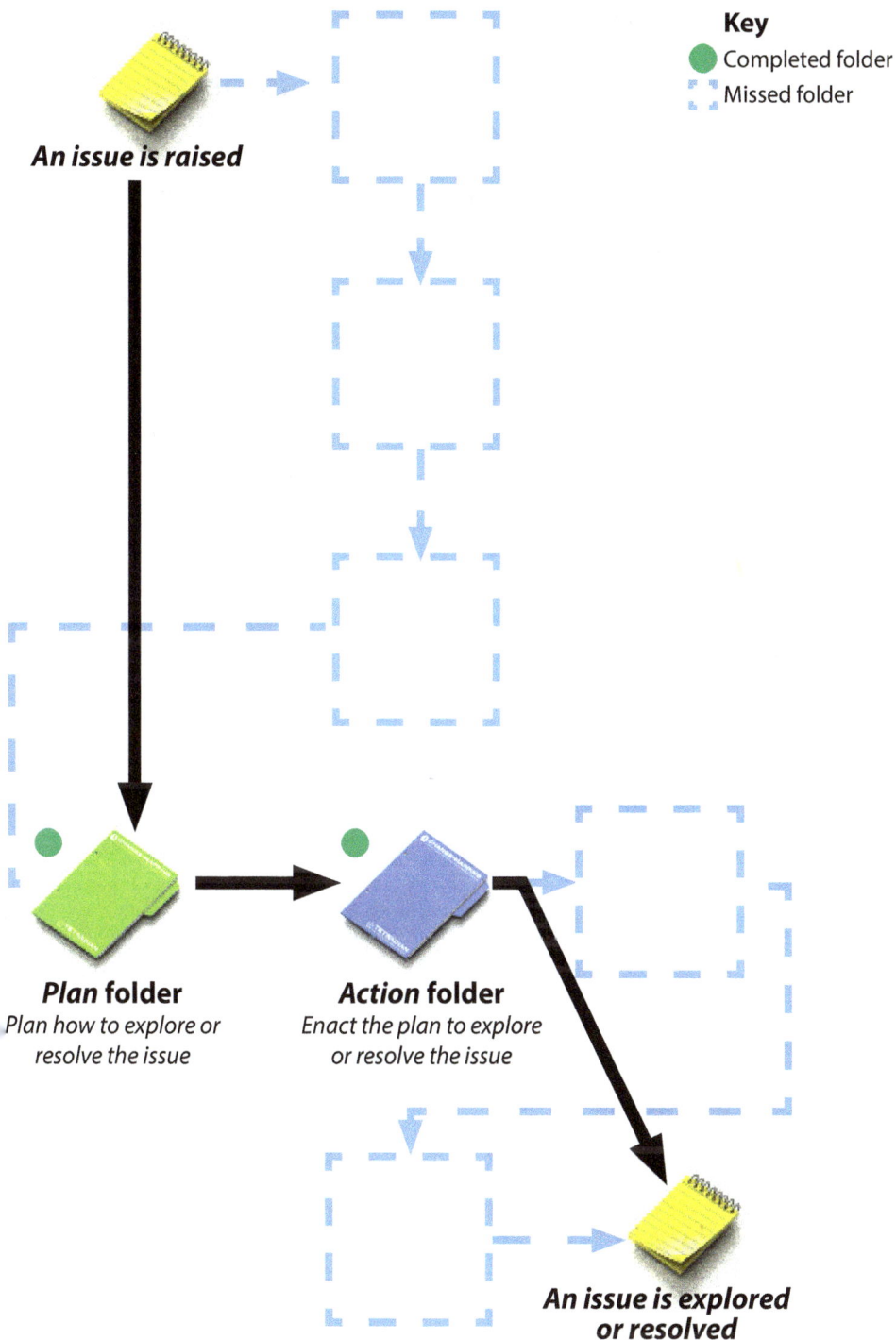

Key
● Completed folder
⬚ Missed folder

An issue is raised

Plan folder
Plan how to explore or resolve the issue

Action folder
Enact the plan to explore or resolve the issue

An issue is explored or resolved

Rushing straight to the plan
While this approach may work, it misses important steps, such as asking "Why does the issue need resolving".

Staying stuck in one part of a mission

Analysis paralysis, office politics and more

Further reading
Thinking, Fast and Slow
by Daniel Kahneman
*Crucial Conversations Tools
for Talking When Stakes
Are High*
by Kerry Patterson
*Corporate Strategy:
Tools for Analysis
and Decision-Making*
by Phanish Puranam

This problem is the opposite of rushing into one part of a mission. Here a team will progress through a mission and then grind to a halt. Most of these issues such as analysis paralysis and office politics can be traced to decision making. With analysis paralysis a team believes they need to do just one more bit of analysis, with the result that nothing actually is changed. And with office politics people will argue over favoured approaches but often the issue still stays unresolved.

These types of problems can be countered by strong unbiased leadership and firm decision making using all available information.

10 minute exercise

"We can't decide!"

In this simple exercise a small team imagine they are on a tiny island which may soon be swamped by the ocean. They can stay where they are, where there is food and water or they can try to swim for a nearby island which is not flooding but may not have food and water.
They can't bring the food and water with them.
What should they do? The exercise looks in brief about making decisions with limited information and time.

An issue is raised

Mission Start folder
*Setup a mission to resolve
or explore the issue*

Context folder
Set the issue in context

Scope folder
*Explore options for action to explore
or resolve the issue*

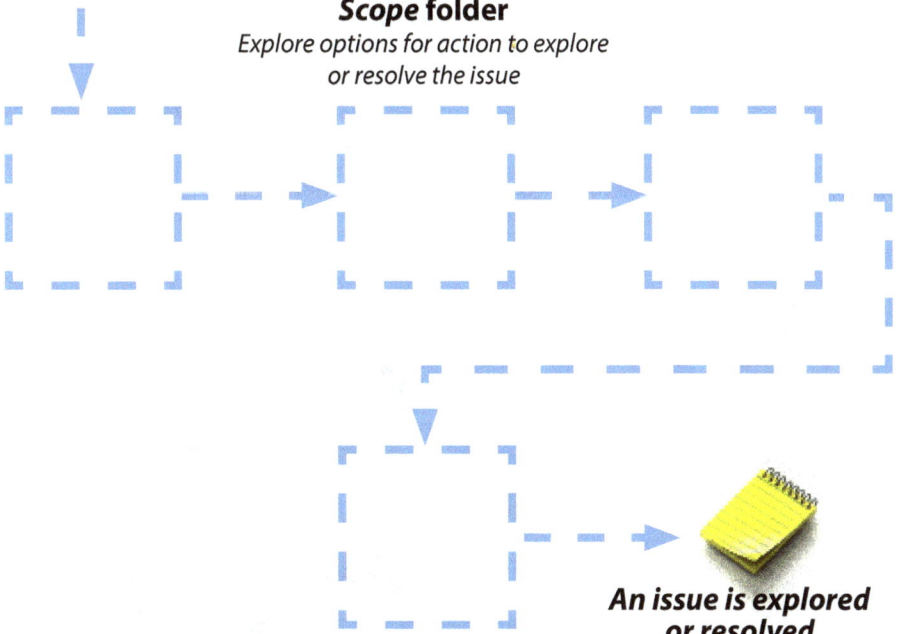

**An issue is explored
or resolved**

Staying stuck in one part of a mission
Here a mission reaches the Scope folder and then grinds to a halt.
Until this is resolved the mission can't be completed.

How much information do we need?

I don't know, it depends and with just enough detail

Further reading
Storytelling with Data:
A Data Visualization Guide
for Business Professionals
by Cole Nussbaumer
Knaflic
Information is Beautiful
by David McCandless

When exploring or resolving an issue one of the main tasks is to gather ideas, information and insights. At the start of a mission typically a team will look at a *wide* range of parts connected to the issue in *low* detail. As the team proceeds through the mission they will look at *narrower* range of parts in *higher* detail. In a similar way to drawing a picture the artist will sketch out the main parts to make sure that everything fits and then add detail to selected areas. The same approach is suggested when trying to explore or resolve an issue.

10 minute exercise

"How much detail do we need?"
This exercise aims to highlight levels of detail.
Ask one person to describe how to open a drinks bottle.
Part one looks at what is the **least** amount of information required to get the bottle open.
Part two looks at what is the **most** amount of information available to get the bottle open. You can go into incredible amounts of detail about the the torsion forces required to remove the lid without breaking the bottle for example. The point of the exercise is to assess how much detail is required to find out what you need. Not too little and not too much, just the right amount.

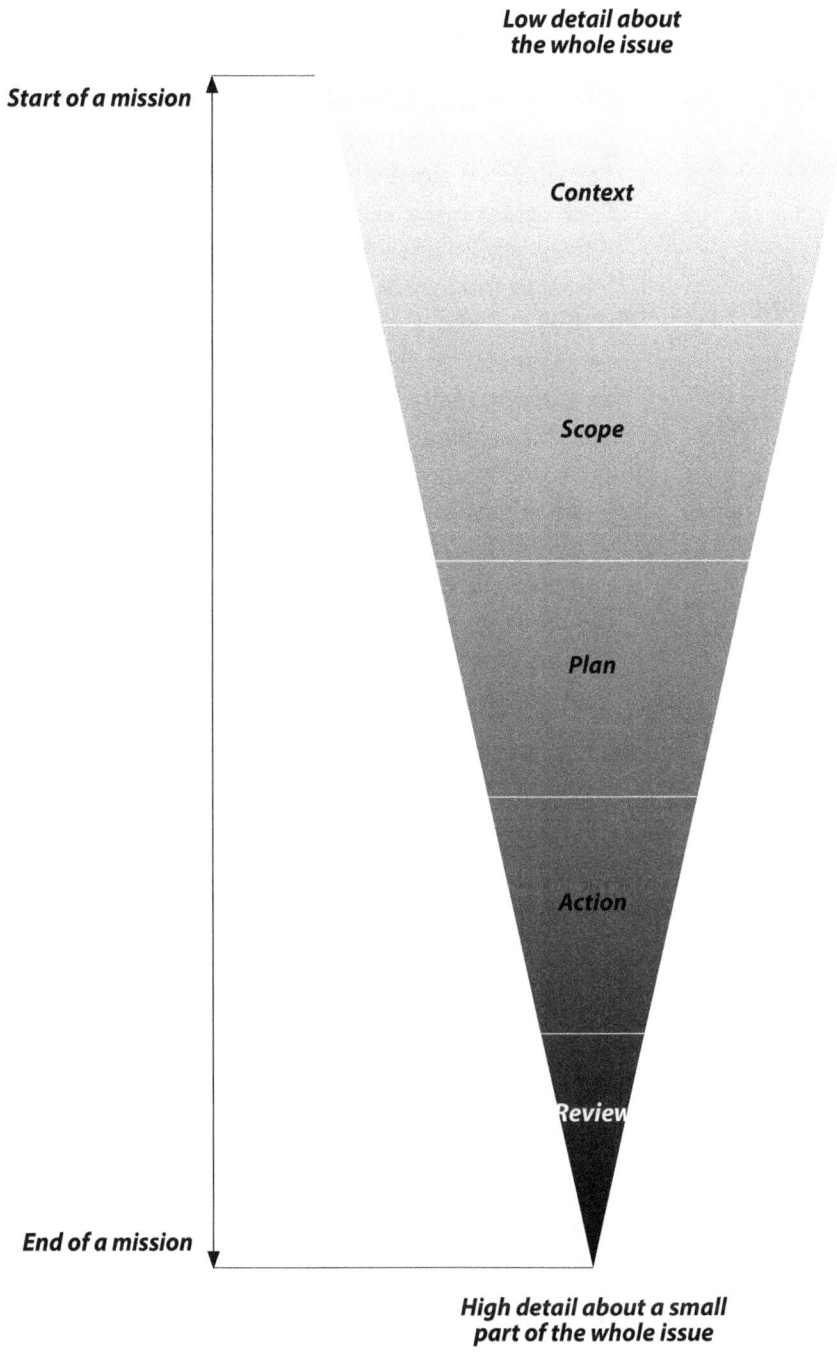

Low detail about
the whole issue

Start of a mission

Context

Scope

Plan

Action

Review

End of a mission

High detail about a small
part of the whole issue

How much information is required
Typically a mission will start in low detail over a wide area and end in high detail over a narrow area.

We can't answer a question!

What happens if you can't find any information?

Further reading
The up coming books by the author will tackle this issue in more depth.
Change-mapping tools
will be a collection of tool-sheets designed to be used in a wide range of issues with clear instructions of when and how to use them.

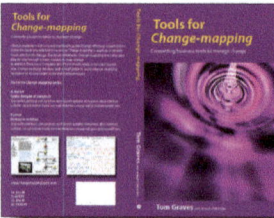

Advanced Change-mapping *will look in more depth about using Change-mapping, with more detailed tools and analysis for more complex issues.*

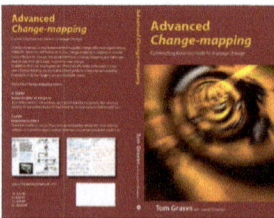

Change-mapping **missions use tool-sheets to find information to explore or resolve an issue. The diagram right shows how this works in detail. Each folder has a set of tool-sheets with questions. If they *can* be answered then move to the next folder in the mission.**

If they *can't* be answered then the question can be skipped *(stating why)*. Or the team can choose an *Existing tool* as shown on *page 112*. These are more specialised tools that can help obtain more detailed information.

If the question still can't be answered after using a specialised tool then a *Nested-mission* is another option available. *Nested missions* work exactly the same way as missions except they are focused on one piece of information. More about *Nested-Missions* can be found on page 114.

10 minute exercise
"Down the rabbit hole"
Run a simple mission to explore why a business might want to invest in new equipment. What is your standard approach to finding out information? Do you find that finding out one piece of information can dominate the whole mission?
How do you decide that you should abandon a particular question and move on to a different question?

Key

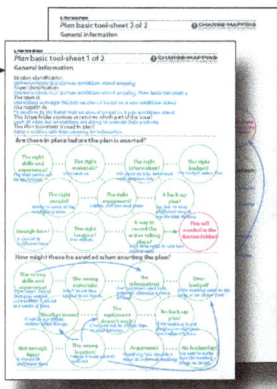

- 🔴 Incomplete folder
- 🟠 Folder in-progress
- 🟢 Completed folder

An issue is raised

Mission Start folder

Can we answer all the tool-sheet questions?

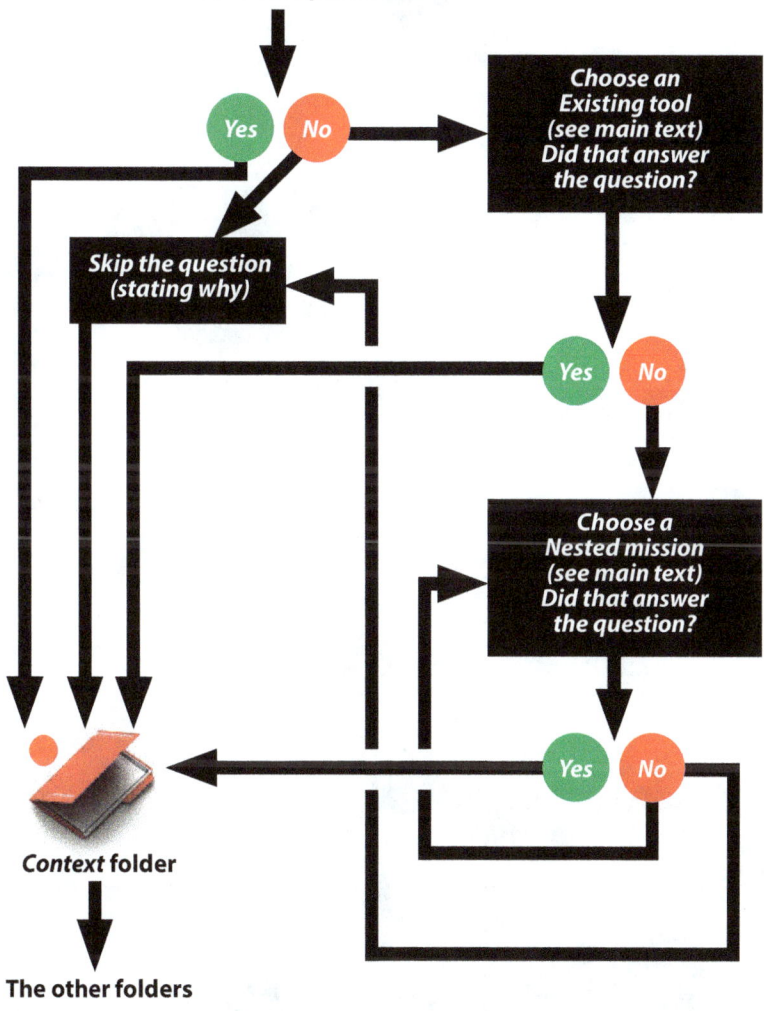

🟢 **Yes**　🔴 **No**

Choose an Existing tool (see main text) Did that answer the question?

Skip the question (stating why)

🟢 **Yes**　🔴 **No**

Choose a Nested mission (see main text) Did that answer the question?

🟢 **Yes**　🔴 **No**

Context folder

The other folders

A more detailed view of how Change-mapping works.

The options available when attempting to find information about an issue.

Part 2:
The basic *Change-mapping* tool-sheets

A complete set of basic *Change-mapping* tool-sheets, with guides how to use them, when exploring or resolving change issues.

Chapter 5: The *Mission Start* tool-sheets
Setting up a mission to explore or resolve an issue

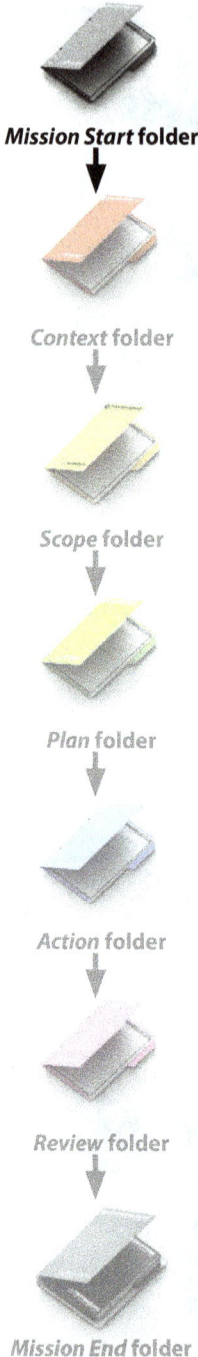

CHANGE→MAPPING
CONNECTING BUSINESS TOOLS TO MANAGE CHANGE

Mission Start folder

↓

Context folder

↓

Scope folder

↓

Plan folder

↓

Action folder

↓

Review folder

↓

Mission End folder

A mission will need a small amount of setup so that everyone knows who is doing what and how.

The basic **Mission Start** tool-sheets do this with two tool-sheets which look at a few main areas:

Tool-sheet 1 asks a few setup questions such as: what is the issue, what type of mission it is and other similar questions. An important thing to note is the type of mission. It might be assumed that it is a mission to resolve the issue, when in fact the mission may be to explore the issue before resolving it.

Tool-sheet 2 acts as a map for the mission. It is filled in by the Observer and shows where the team is inside a mission and what the state of the mission is.

How to use the tool-sheets
General instructions

These tool-sheets are designed to be used by a small team of 4-12 **Explorers*** to capture ideas, information and insights during a mission. A **Pathfinder*** will make sure the Explorers stay on the task, while allowing unexpected insights to occur. An **Observer*** will note down all the teams findings on the tool-sheets and additional paper if required.

Each tool-sheet has a general information section which is used to identify the issue, mission and the tool-sheet itself. The basic *Mission Start* tool-sheets are made up of a set of two tool-sheets.

Each section of the tool-sheet with circles asks the team to describe the issue and its context. The circles are not meant to be answered in any order, but rather to start conversations. The questions in the circles are not meant to cover every possible question, but rather the team can add their own context specific questions to the generic questions.

The *Mission Start 2* tool-sheet is a map of the whole mission which should be filled in as the mission progresses. This will show what has been done and what still needs to be completed. This helps when people are unsure where they are within a mission.

*See page 12 about the roles in Change-mapping.

Mission Start basic tool-sheet 1 of 2   ⓘ CHANGE-MAPPING

General information

Mission identification:
Shirmin/0001/2.2.22/new exhibition stand enquiry
Sheet identification:
Shirmin/0001/2.2.22/new exhibition stand enquiry/Mission Start basic tool-sheet 1

Mission setup...

The company needs a new exhibition stand. We have a new product which needs to be promoted.

- What is the issue?
- Who raised the issue?
  The marketing manager
- Who is the decision maker for what is found in the mission?
  The board of directors
- Who requested the mission?
  The board of directors
- Who is the mission commander?
  Head of Strategy will commit mission
- Who are the: Explorers? Pathfinder? Observer?
  4 Explorers spread across the organisation. Pathfinder and Observer from marketing.
- Mission duration and budget?
  The board will require an answer within one week. Budget includes staff
- What are the deliverables for the mission?
  A definitive answer if we should or shouldn't invest in a new exhibition stand.
- How will the information be: stored, shared and retrieved?
  The Observer will store the information on our local server and will distribute to those require it.

This currently is a single mission, but based on what we find it may be the first of a set of linked missions.

What type of mission will be undertaken...

This mission will be to explore if we need a new exhibition stand. The marketing manager wants a way to promote our new forest management system.

This currently is a single mission, but based on what we find it may be the first of a set of linked missions.

- A mission to explore the issue
- A mission to resolve the issue
- A mission linked to other missions

We thought the mission was to find out how to invest in a new exhibition stand. But we haven't explored if we should invest in a new exhibition stand.

Mission Start basic tool-sheet 1 of 2   ⓘ CHANGE-MAPPING

General information

Mission identification:
Sheet identification:

Mission setup...

- What is the issue?
- Who raised the issue?
- Who is the decision maker for what is found in the mission?
- Who requested the mission?
- Who is the mission commander?
- Who are the: Explorers? Pathfinder? Observer?
- Mission duration and budget?
- What are the deliverables for the mission?
- How will the information be: stored, shared and retrieved?

What type of mission will be undertaken...

- A mission to explore the issue
- A mission to resolve the issue
- A mission linked to other missions

Mission Start basic tool-sheet 2 of 2   ⓘ CHANGE-MAPPING

General information

Mission identification:
Shirmin/0001/2.2.22/new exhibition stand enquiry
Sheet identification:
Shirmin/0001/2.2.22/new exhibition stand enquiry/context basic tool-sheet 1
The issue is:
Marketing manager believes we should invest in a new exhibition stand.
Our mission is:
To confirm to the board whether we should invest in a new exhibition stand.

A record of the mission

Key
- 🔴 Incomplete folder
- 🟠 Folder in-progress
- 🟢 Completed folder
- ❌ Folder abandoned

We set up the mission parameters

Mission Start Folder

We explored how the issue fits into our organisation, our customers and beyond.

Here we explored potential visitor members to the FM show. They were not what we expected.

Context Folder

Scope Folder

Here we explored other ways of promoting our system, which was why we had considered a stand.

Scope Folder

Plan Folder   Action Folder   Review Folder

Mission End Portfolio

Scope Folder

Here we were going to explore the cost of a new stand. But we decided not to explore further after what was found earlier.

Here we reviewed the whole mission and decided what to do next.

Mission Start basic tool-sheet 2 of 2   ⓘ CHANGE-MAPPING

General information

Mission identification:
Sheet identification:
The issue is:
Our mission is:

A record of the mission

Key
- 🔴 Incomplete folder
- 🟠 Folder in-progress
- 🟢 Completed folder
- ❌ Folder abandoned

To show how the tool-sheets are used on the left one is filled in with a worked example.
On the right is a blank version which can be photocopied for your own projects.

Mission Start basic tool-sheet 1 of 2

CHANGE→MAPPING
CONNECTING BUSINESS TOOLS TO MANAGE CHANGE

General information

Mission identification:
Shirnrin/0001/2.2.22/new exhibition stand enquiry
Sheet identification:
Shirnrin/0001/2.2.22/new exhibition stand enquiry, Mission Start basic tool-sheet 1

Mission setup...

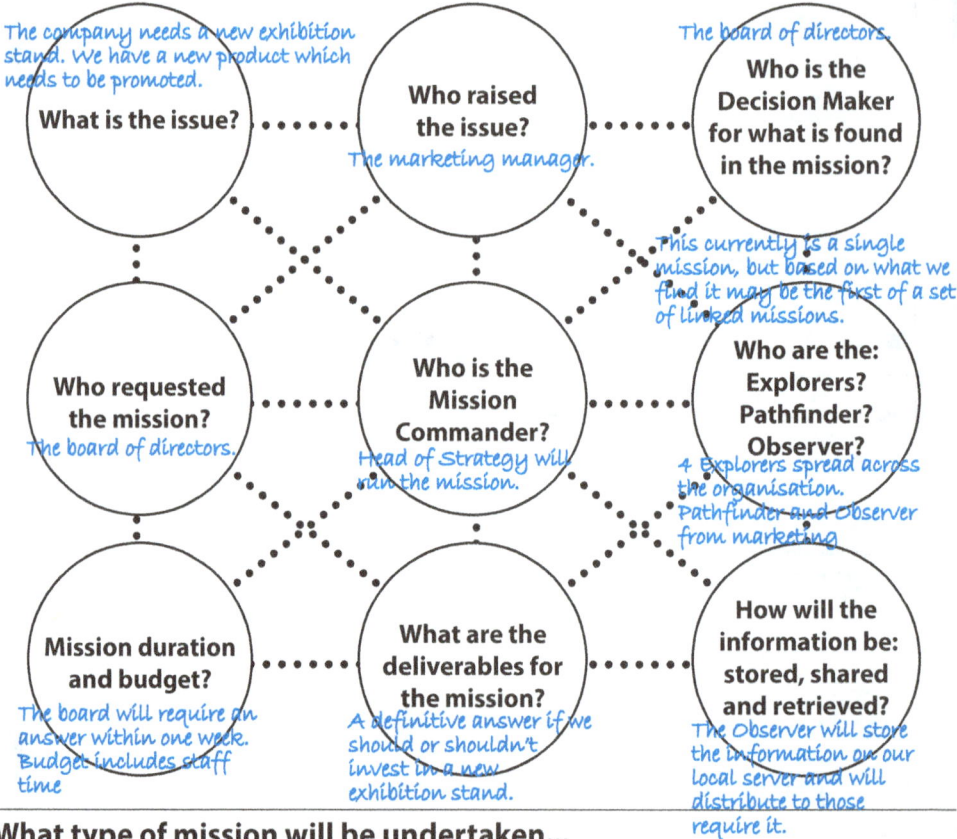

What is the issue?
The company needs a new exhibition stand. We have a new product which needs to be promoted.

Who raised the issue?
The marketing manager.

Who is the Decision Maker for what is found in the mission?
The board of directors.

Who requested the mission?
The board of directors.

Who is the Mission Commander?
Head of Strategy will run the mission.

Who are the: Explorers? Pathfinder? Observer?
This currently is a single mission, but based on what we find it may be the first of a set of linked missions.
4 Explorers spread across the organisation. Pathfinder and Observer from marketing

Mission duration and budget?
The board will require an answer within one week. Budget includes staff time

What are the deliverables for the mission?
A definitive answer if we should or shouldn't invest in a new exhibition stand.

How will the information be: stored, shared and retrieved?
The Observer will store the information on our local server and will distribute to those require it.

What type of mission will be undertaken...

This mission will be to explore if we need a new exhibition stand. The marketing manager wants a way to promote our new forest management system.

This currently is a single mission, but based on what we find it may be the first of a set of linked missions.

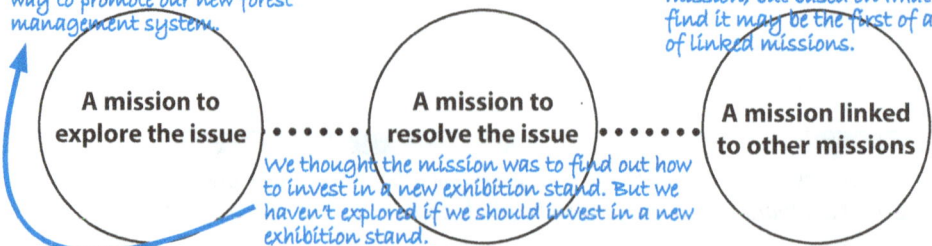

A mission to explore the issue

A mission to resolve the issue
We thought the mission was to find out how to invest in a new exhibition stand. But we haven't explored if we should invest in a new exhibition stand.

A mission linked to other missions

CHANGE→MAPPING
CONNECTING BUSINESS TOOLS TO MANAGE CHANGE

General information

Mission identification:

Sheet identification:

Mission setup...

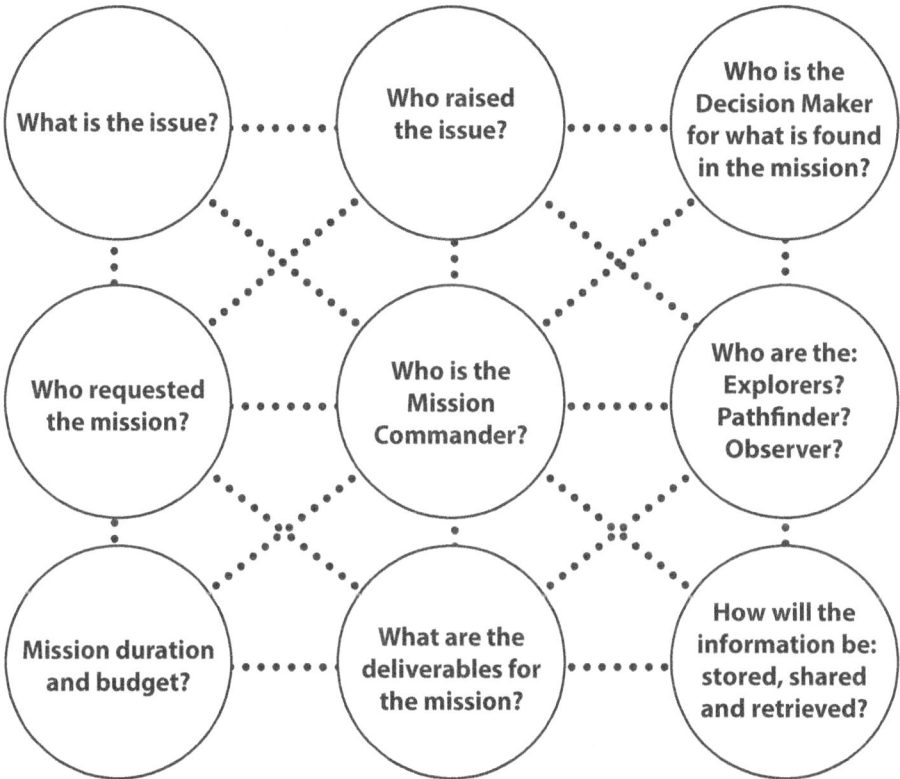

What is the issue? • • • • • Who raised the issue? • • • • • • Who is the Decision Maker for what is found in the mission?

Who requested the mission? • • • • • • Who is the Mission Commander? • • • • • • Who are the: Explorers? Pathfinder? Observer?

Mission duration and budget? • • • • • • What are the deliverables for the mission? • • • • • • How will the information be: stored, shared and retrieved?

What type of mission will be undertaken...

A mission to explore the issue • • • • • • A mission to resolve the issue • • • • • • A mission linked to other missions

Mission Start basic tool-sheet 2 of 2

CHANGE+MAPPING
CONNECTING BUSINESS TOOLS TO MANAGE CHANGE

General information

Mission identification:
Shirnrin/0001/2.2.22/new exhibition stand enquiry
Sheet identification:
Shirnrin/0001/2.2.22/new exhibition stand enquiry, context basic tool-sheet 1
The issue is:
Marketing manager believes we should invest in a new exhibition stand.
Our mission is:
To confirm to the board whether we should invest in a new exhibition stand.

A record of the mission

We set up the mission parameters

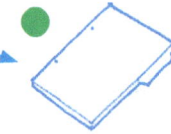

Key
- 🔴 Incomplete folder
- 🟠 Folder in-progress
- 🟢 Completed folder
- ❌ Folder abandoned

Mission Start
Folder

We explored how the issue fits into our organisation, our customers and beyond.

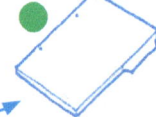

Here we explored potential visitor numbers to the FM show. They were not what we expected.

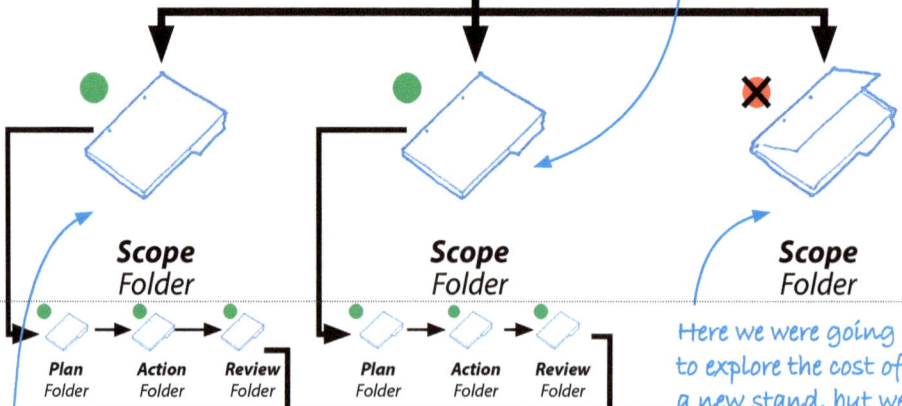

Context
Folder

Scope
Folder

| **Plan** | **Action** | **Review** |
| Folder | Folder | Folder |

Scope
Folder

| **Plan** | **Action** | **Review** |
| Folder | Folder | Folder |

Scope
Folder

Here we were going to explore the cost of a new stand, but we decided not to explore further after what was found earlier.

Here we explored other ways of promoting our system, which was why we had considered a stand.

Mission End
Portfolio

Here we reviewed the whole mission and decided what to do next.

CHANGE→MAPPING
CONNECTING BUSINESS TOOLS TO MANAGE CHANGE

General information

Mission identification:

Sheet identification:

The issue is:

Our mission is:

A record of the mission

Key
🔴 Incomplete folder
🟠 Folder in-progress
🟢 Completed folder
✖ Folder abandoned

Chapter 6: The *Context* tool-sheets

Setting the issue in context

CHANGE→MAPPING
CONNECTING BUSINESS TOOLS TO MANAGE CHANGE

Mission Start folder

↓

Context folder

↓

Scope folder

↓

Plan folder

↓

Action folder

↓

Review folder

↓

Mission End folder

If your organisation faces an unknown issue affected by change, then setting the issue in context can be vital. Rather than rushing straight to a solution which potentially can be solving the wrong thing, *Context* tool-sheets are used to map out the issue and set it in context.

The basic *Context* tool-sheets do this with four tool-sheets which look at a few main areas:

Tool-sheet 1 examines the issue itself and sets it in context.

Tool-sheet 2 looks at how standards, regulations and laws might affect any solution devised by a team to explore or resolve the issue.

Tool-sheet 3 asks what will take priority when any plan is being enacted.

Tool-sheet 4 investigates how plans and actions will be reviewed and which areas of the issue will be explored further

How to use the tool-sheets.

General instructions

These tool-sheets are designed to be used by a small team of 4-12 **Explorers*** to capture ideas, information and insights during a mission. A **Pathfinder** will make sure the Explorers stay on the task, while allowing unexpected insights to occur. An **Observer** will note down all the teams findings on the tool-sheets and additional paper if required.

Each tool-sheet has a general information section which is used to identify the issue, mission and the tool-sheet itself.

The basic *Context* tool-sheets are made up of a set of four tool sheets. It is recommended to fill out all four to obtain a broad view of the context and possible factors which can influence any potential solutions.

Each section of the tool-sheet with circles asks the team to describe the issue and its context. The circles are not meant to be answered in any order, but rather start conversations.

The questions in the circles are not meant to cover every possible question, but rather the team can add their own context specific questions to the generic questions.

At the end of the basic *Context* tool-sheets a broad picture should appear about the issue and its context. As well gaps which the team want to explore or resolve further should become apparent. Each of these will have its own *Scope* folder used to work out how to resolve or explore that one part of the context.

*See page 12 about the roles in Change-mapping.

Context basic tool-sheet 1 of 4   ● CHANGE-MAPPING

General information

Mission identification:
Shimrin/0001/2.2.22/new exhibition stand enquiry
Sheet identification:
Shimrin/0001/2.2.22/new exhibition stand enquiry.context basic tool-sheet 1
The issue is:
Marketing manager believes we should invest in a new exhibition stand.
Our mission is:
To confirm to the board that we should invest in a new exhibition stand.

Describing the issue...

Why does it happen? — We have a new product and we need to promote it.
What happens? — We need an effective way to launch our product, so a stand was suggested.
Where does it happen? — Our industry standard show is in Seattle in two months, many contacts will be there.
Why does it need to be solved? — We need to make people aware of our new product, otherwise all that effort will be wasted.
Who is it happening to? — Our organisation need an effective way to promote the new product.
When does it happen? — The new product is ready to be launched now.
How does it happen? — We are not sure an exhibition stand is the best way to promote the new product.

How is the issue affected by...

Our organisation — We know that we are sure if it is the most effective method.
Our clients — Some of our clients visit trade shows but others prefer face to face meetings.
Our suppliers — If our current exhibition stand manufacturer is available to build a stand.
Our competitors — Many of our competitors exhibit at the trade shows.
Time — The exhibition is in two months.
Weather — Delivering the exhibition might be tricky with spring floods.
Sustainability — Can we reuse the stand for other shows?
Politics — The uncertain political climate makes any big investment a risk.
Economics — We need to buy things to the last minute which will raise the initial price.
Social — We need to be seen so is making a difference.
Technology — Maybe a upgraded website would be more effective?
Our industry — We work in forest management which is facing huge change.
Information — We should find out what our competitors are doing.
World events — Our industry is hugely affected by the ongoing bush-fires.

Context basic tool-sheet 1 of 4   ● CHANGE-MAPPING

General information

Mission identification:

Sheet identification:

The issue is:

Our mission is:

Describing the issue...

Why does it happen?
What happens?
Where does it happen?
Why does it need to be solved?
Who is it happening to?
When does it happen?
How does it happen?

How is the issue affected by...

Our organisation
Our clients
Our suppliers
Our competitors
Time
Weather
Sustainability
Politics
Economics
Social
Technology
Our industry
Information
World events

Context basic tool-sheet 4 of 4   ● CHANGE-MAPPING

General information

Mission identification:
Shimrin/0001/2.2.22/new exhibition stand enquiry
Sheet identification:
Shimrin/0001/2.2.22/new exhibition stand enquiry.context basic tool-sheet 4
The issue is:
Marketing manager believes we should invest in a new exhibition stand.
Our mission is:
To confirm to the board that we should invest in a new exhibition stand.

When a plan has been enacted, how will it be judged against...

Our organisation — We need an effective way to measure success.
Health & safety — A new exhibition of the plan, we need to make any plan for risk.
Sustainability — How will we measure this? Carbon neutral, no plastic waste?
Short term — Once a week review of all activities?
Long term — Once every six months strategy review?
Value — Value to us that: more know about our product and to the silent that they can make an informed choice.
Time — Once a week review of all activities?
Quality — If our message has lead to an increase in sales?
This will be needed in the Review folder — We need effective success criteria that can be measured in some way.

List which parts of the Context will be explored further or resolved.

Explore or resolve this part... — Look at what our competitors are doing to promote their products.
Explore or resolve this part... — Find out the cost of an exhibition stand from our usual supplier.
Explore or resolve this part... — What do our clients respond to in terms of marketing?
This part will have its own Scope folder — We would need a rough drawing of what we want after first?
This part will have its own Scope folder
This part will have its own Scope folder

Context basic tool-sheet 4 of 4   ● CHANGE-MAPPING

General information

Mission identification:

Sheet identification:

The issue is:

Our mission is:

When a plan has been enacted, how will it be judged against...

Our organisation
Health & safety
Sustainability
Short term
Long term
Value
Time
Quality
This will be needed in the Review folder

List which parts of the Context will be explored further or resolved.

Explore or resolve this part...
Explore or resolve this part...
Explore or resolve this part...
This part will have its own Scope folder
This part will have its own Scope folder
This part will have its own Scope folder

To show how the tool-sheets are used on the left one is filled in with a worked example.
On the right is a blank version which can be photocopied for your own projects.

Context basic tool-sheet 1 of 4

CHANGE→MAPPING
CONNECTING BUSINESS TOOLS TO MANAGE CHANGE

General information

Mission identification:
Shirnrin/0001/2.2.22/new exhibition stand enquiry
Sheet identification:
Shirnrin/0001/2.2.22/new exhibition stand enquiry, context basic tool-sheet 1
The issue is:
Marketing manager believes we should invest in a new exhibition stand.
Our mission is:
To confirm to the board whether we should invest in a new exhibition stand.

Describing the issue...

We have a new product and we need to promote it.

Why does it happen?

We need an effective way to launch our product, so a stand was suggested.

What happens?

Our industry standard show is in Seattle in two months, many contacts will be there.

Where does it happen?

We need to make peopl aware of our new produ otherwise all that effor be wasted.

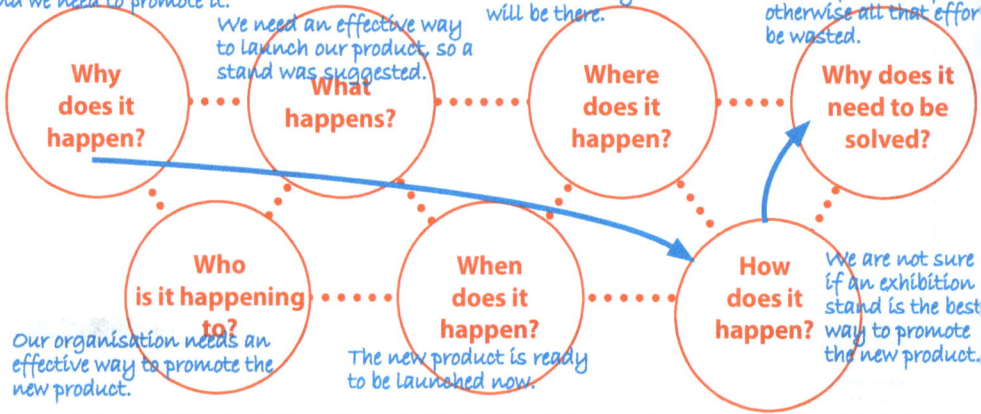

Why does it need to be solved?

Who is it happening to?

Our organisation needs an effective way to promote the new product.

When does it happen?

The new product is ready to be launched now.

How does it happen?

We are not sure if an exhibition stand is the best way to promote the new product.

How is the issue affected by...

We always exhibit at trade shows, but we are not sure if it is the most effective method.

Our organisation

Some of our clients visit trade shows but others prefer face to face meetings.

Our clients

If our normal exhibition stand manufacturer is available to build a stand?

Our suppliers

Our competitors

Many of our competit exhibit at the trade sho

Time

The exhibition is in two months.

Weather

Delivering the exhibition might be tricky with spring floods.

Sustainability

Can we reuse the stand for other shows?

Politics

The uncertain political climate makes any big investment a risk.

Economics

We have left things to the last minute which will raise the build price.

Social

We need to be seen to be making a difference.

Technology

Maybe a upgraded website would be more effective?

Our industry

We work in forest management which is facing huge change.

Information

We should find out what our competitors are doing.

World events

Our industry is hugely affected by increasing bush-fires.

CHANGE→MAPPING
CONNECTING BUSINESS TOOLS TO MANAGE CHANGE

General information

Mission identification:

Sheet identification:

The issue is:

Our mission is:

Describing the issue...

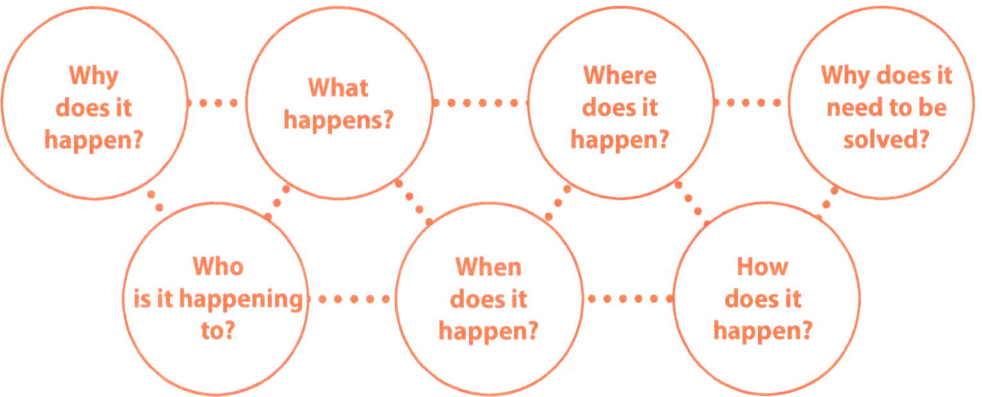

Why does it happen?

What happens?

Where does it happen?

Why does it need to be solved?

Who is it happening to?

When does it happen?

How does it happen?

How is the issue affected by...

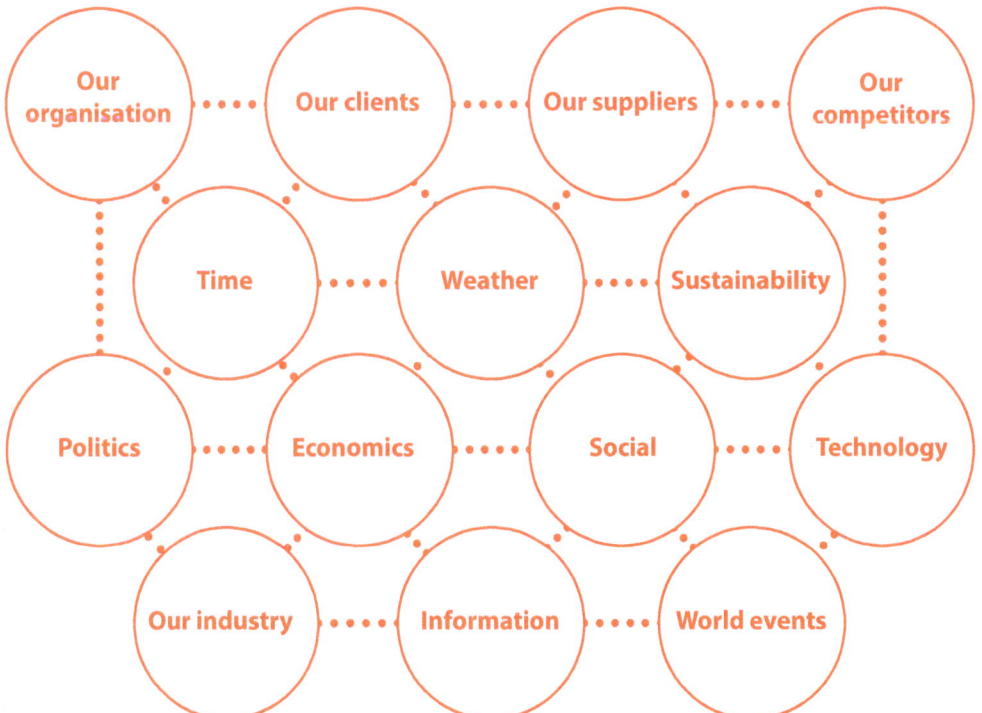

Our organisation

Our clients

Our suppliers

Our competitors

Time

Weather

Sustainability

Politics

Economics

Social

Technology

Our industry

Information

World events

Context basic tool-sheet 2 of 4

CHANGE→MAPPING
CONNECTING BUSINESS TOOLS TO MANAGE CHANGE

General information

Mission identification:
Shirnrin/0001/2.2.22/new exhibition stand enquiry
Sheet identification:
Shirnrin/0001/2.2.22/new exhibition stand enquiry, context basic tool-sheet 2
The issue is:
Marketing manager believes we should invest in a new exhibition stand.
Our mission is:
To confirm to the board whether we should invest in a new exhibition stand.

How could these affect plans to explore or resolve part of the issue...

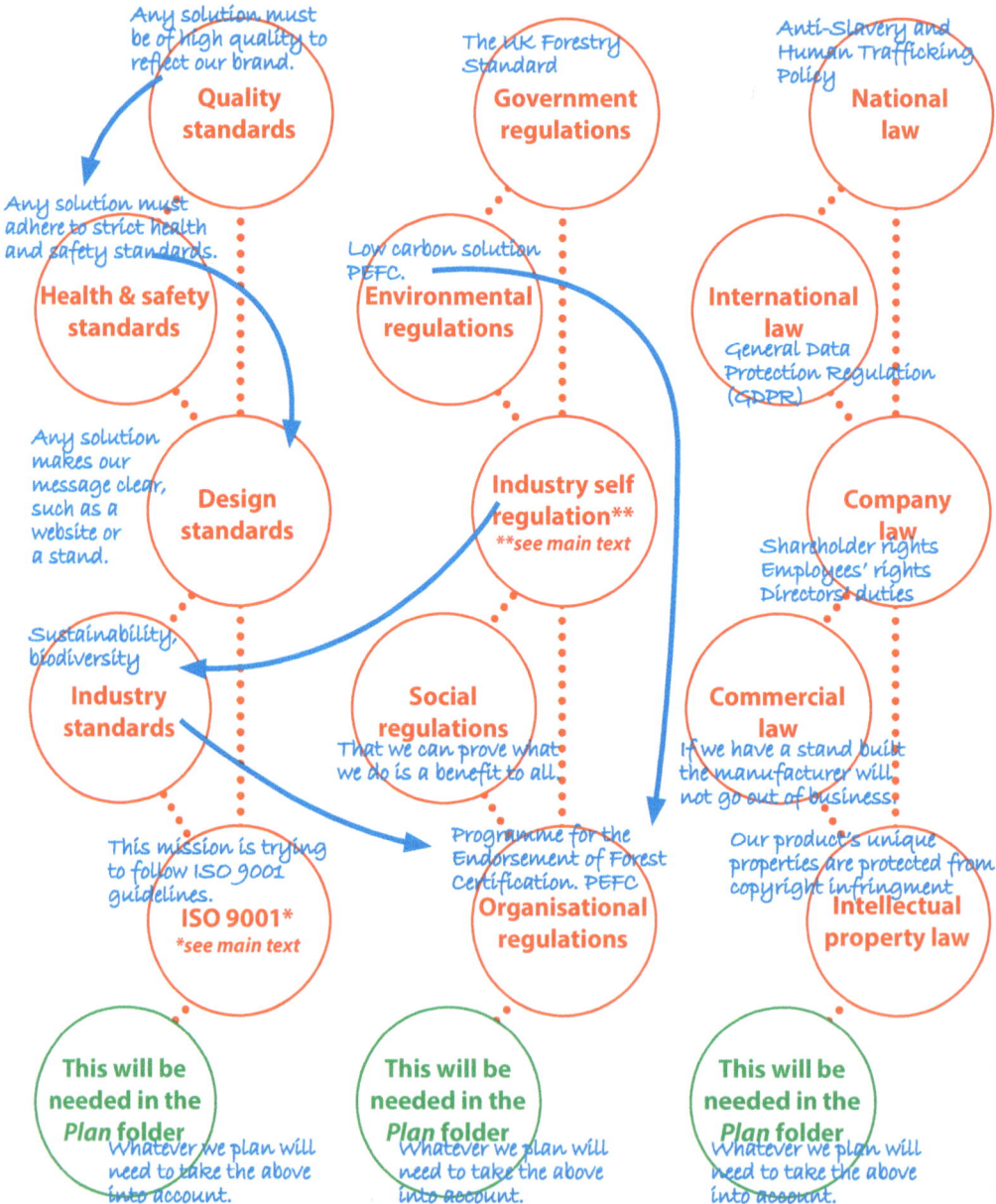

Any solution must be of high quality to reflect our brand.

Quality standards

The UK Forestry Standard

Government regulations

Anti-Slavery and Human Trafficking Policy

National law

Any solution must adhere to strict health and safety standards.

Health & safety standards

Low carbon solution PEFC.

Environmental regulations

International law

General Data Protection Regulation (GDPR)

Any solution makes our message clear, such as a website or a stand.

Design standards

Industry self regulation**
**see main text

Company law

Shareholder rights
Employees' rights
Directors' duties

Sustainability, biodiversity

Industry standards

Social regulations

That we can prove what we do is a benefit to all.

Commercial law

If we have a stand built the manufacturer will not go out of business.

This mission is trying to follow ISO 9001 guidelines.

ISO 9001*
*see main text

Programme for the Endorsement of Forest Certification. PEFC

Organisational regulations

Our product's unique properties are protected from copyright infringment

Intellectual property law

This will be needed in the *Plan* folder
Whatever we plan will need to take the above into account.

This will be needed in the *Plan* folder
Whatever we plan will need to take the above into account.

This will be needed in the *Plan* folder
Whatever we plan will need to take the above into account.

CHANGE→MAPPING
CONNECTING BUSINESS TOOLS TO MANAGE CHANGE

General information

Mission identification:

Sheet identification:

The issue is:

Our mission is:

How could these affect plans to explore or resolve part of the issue...

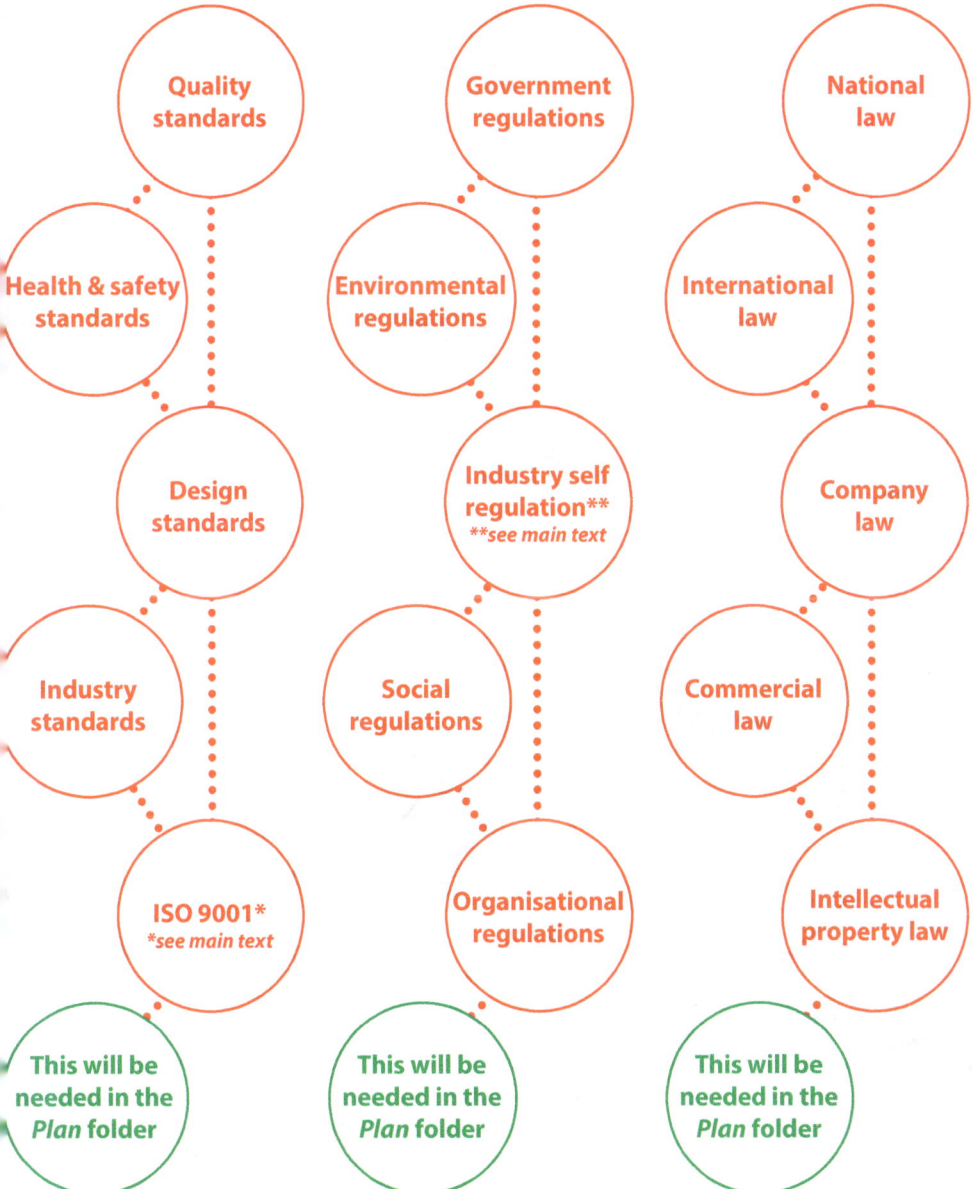

Quality standards

Government regulations

National law

Health & safety standards

Environmental regulations

International law

Design standards

Industry self regulation**
**see main text*

Company law

Industry standards

Social regulations

Commercial law

ISO 9001*
see main text

Organisational regulations

Intellectual property law

This will be needed in the *Plan* folder

This will be needed in the *Plan* folder

This will be needed in the *Plan* folder

Context basic tool-sheet 3 of 4

CHANGE→MAPPING
CONNECTING BUSINESS TOOLS TO MANAGE CHANGE

General information

Mission identification:
Shirnrin/0001/2.2.22/new exhibition stand enquiry
Sheet identification:
Shirnrin/0001/2.2.22/new exhibition stand enquiry,context basic tool-sheet 3
The issue is:
Marketing manager believes we should invest in a new exhibition stand.
Our mission is:
To confirm to the board whether we should invest in a new exhibition stand.

Which of these will take priority when the plan is being enacted?

INSIGHT
What do our clients respond to in terms of marketing?
We want to explore this further with a Scope Folder.

Any last minute changes will lead to extra costs

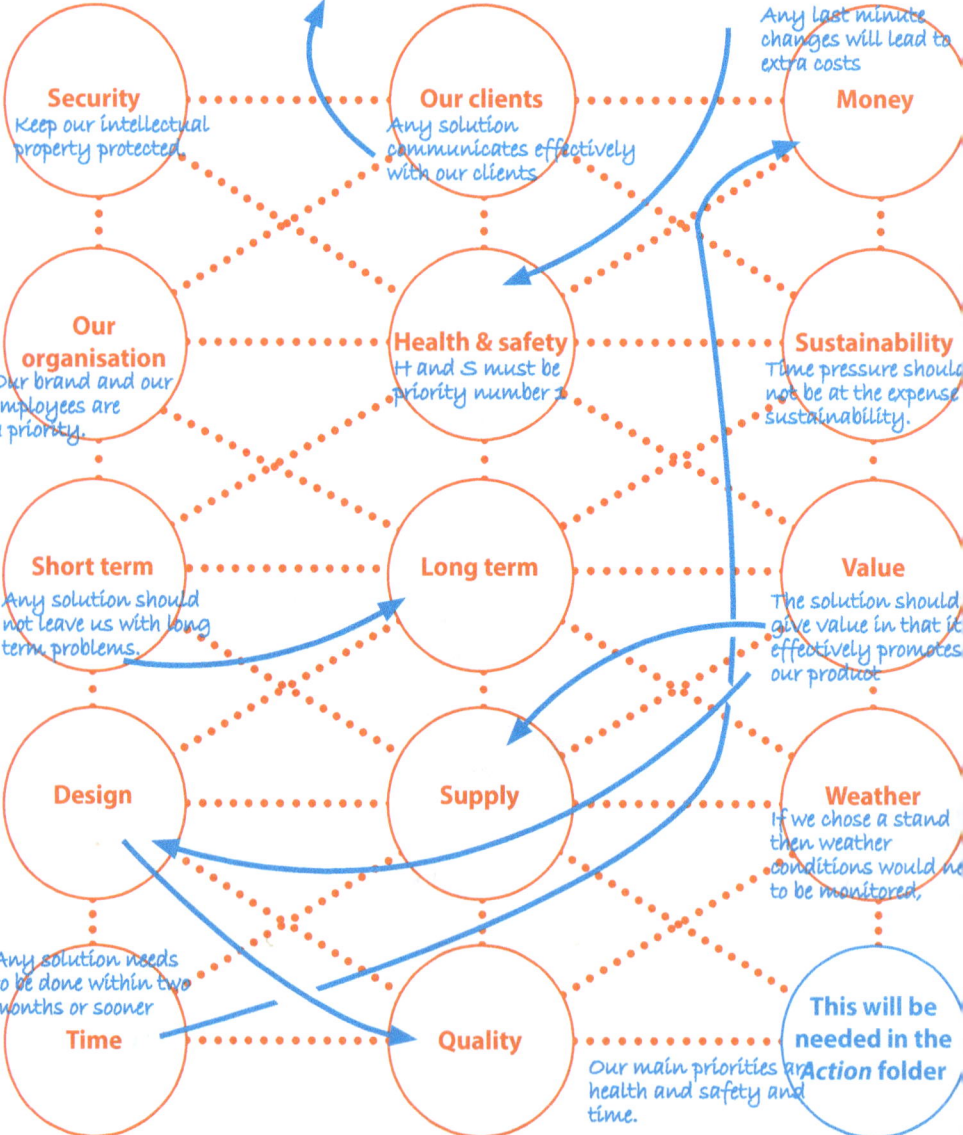

Security
Keep our intellectual property protected.

Our clients
Any solution communicates effectively with our clients

Money

Our organisation
Our brand and our employees are a priority.

Health & safety
H and S must be priority number 1

Sustainability
Time pressure should not be at the expense sustainability.

Short term
Any solution should not leave us with long term problems.

Long term

Value
The solution should give value in that it effectively promotes our product

Design

Supply

Weather
If we chose a stand then weather conditions would need to be monitored.

Any solution needs to be done within two months or sooner

Time

Quality
Our main priorities are health and safety and time.

This will be needed in the Action folder

CHANGE→MAPPING
CONNECTING BUSINESS TOOLS TO MANAGE CHANGE

General information

Mission identification:

Sheet identification:

The issue is:

Our mission is:

Which of these will take priority when the plan is being enacted?

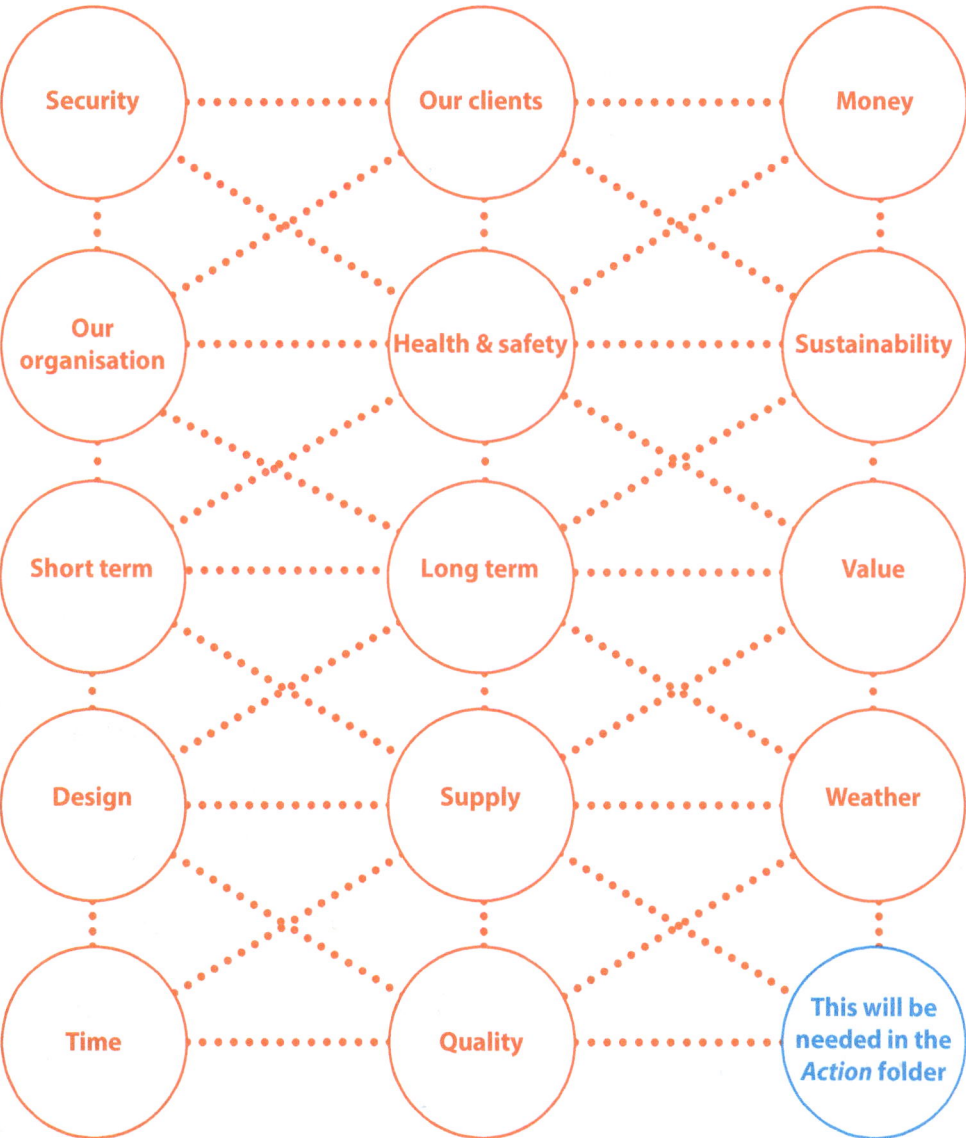

Security	Our clients	Money
Our organisation	Health & safety	Sustainability
Short term	Long term	Value
Design	Supply	Weather
Time	Quality	This will be needed in the *Action* folder

Context basic tool-sheet 4 of 4

CHANGE→MAPPING
CONNECTING BUSINESS TOOLS TO MANAGE CHANGE

General information

Mission identification:
Shirmin/0001/2.2.22/new exhibition stand enquiry
Sheet identification:
Shirmin/0001/2.2.22/new exhibition stand enquiry, context basic tool-sheet 4
The issue is:
Marketing manager believes we should invest in a new exhibition stand.
Our mission is:
To confirm to the board whether we should invest in a new exhibition stand.

When a plan has been enacted, how will it be judged against...

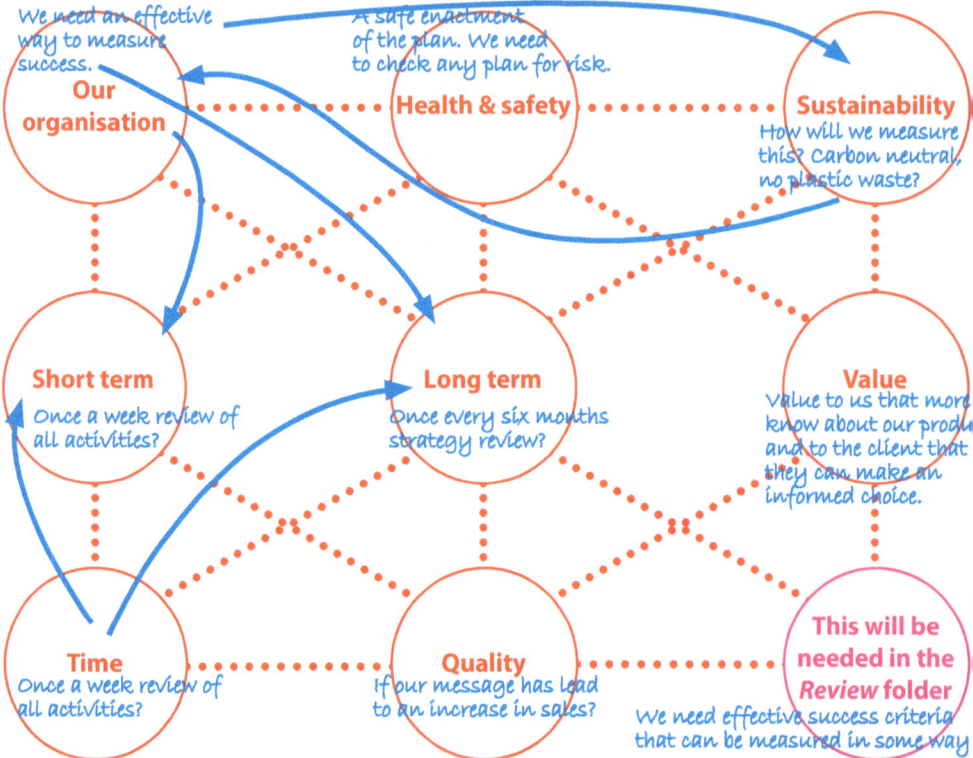

We need an effective way to measure success.

Our organisation

A safe enactment of the plan. We need to check any plan for risk.

Health & safety

Sustainability
How will we measure this? Carbon neutral, no plastic waste?

Short term
Once a week review of all activities?

Long term
Once every six months strategy review?

Value
Value to us that more know about our product and to the client that they can make an informed choice.

Time
Once a week review of all activities?

Quality
If our message has lead to an increase in sales?

This will be needed in the *Review* folder
We need effective success criteria that can be measured in some way

List which parts of the Context will be explored further or resolved.

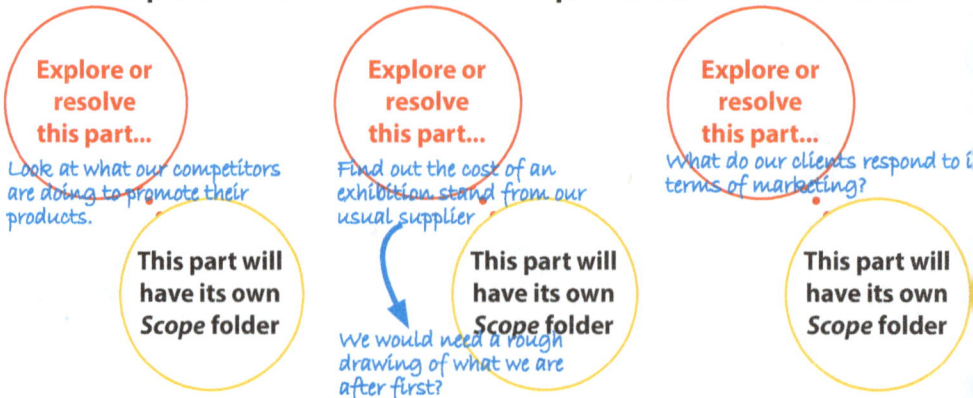

Explore or resolve this part...
Look at what our competitors are doing to promote their products.

Explore or resolve this part...
Find out the cost of an exhibition stand from our usual supplier

Explore or resolve this part...
What do our clients respond to in terms of marketing?

This part will have its own *Scope* folder

This part will have its own *Scope* folder
We would need a rough drawing of what we are after first?

This part will have its own *Scope* folder

Context **basic tool-sheet 4 of 4**

◑ CHANGE→MAPPING
CONNECTING BUSINESS TOOLS TO MANAGE CHANGE

General information

Mission identification:

Sheet identification:

The issue is:

Our mission is:

When a plan has been enacted, how will it be judged against...

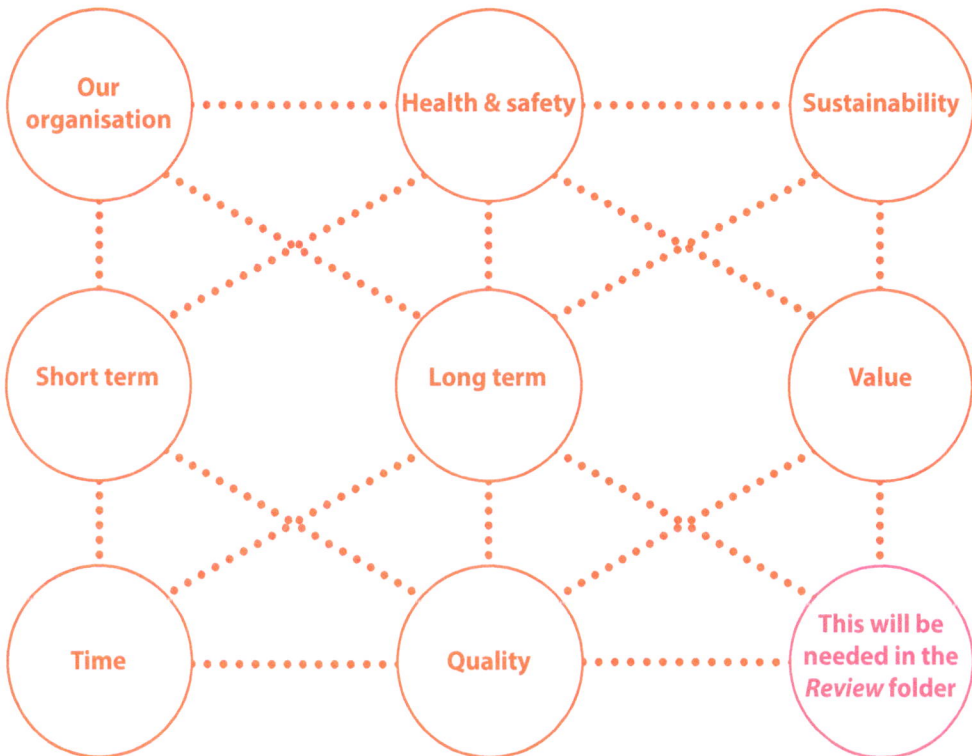

Our organisation · · · · · · · Health & safety · · · · · · · Sustainability

Short term   Long term   Value

Time · · · · · · · Quality · · · · · · · This will be needed in the *Review* folder

---

List which parts of the Context will be explored further or resolved.

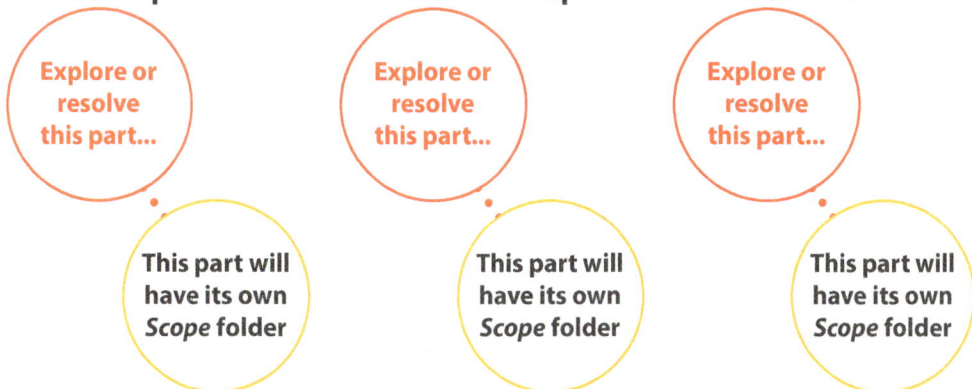

Explore or resolve this part...

Explore or resolve this part...

Explore or resolve this part...

This part will have its own *Scope* folder

This part will have its own *Scope* folder

This part will have its own *Scope* folder

Chapter 7: The *Scope* tool-sheets
Choosing options to explore or resolve part of the issue

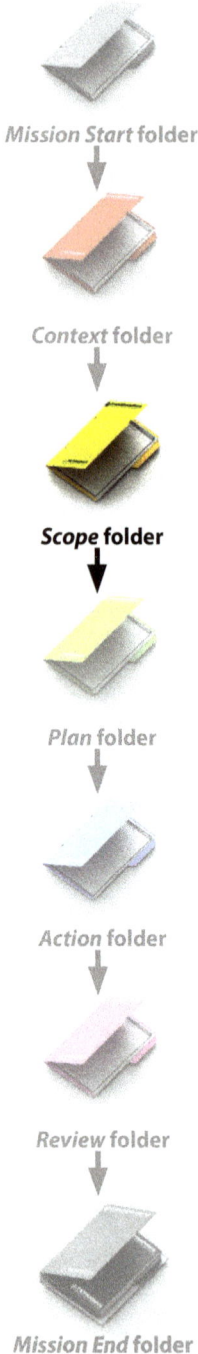

CHANGE→MAPPING
CONNECTING BUSINESS TOOLS TO MANAGE CHANGE

Mission Start folder

↓

Context folder

↓

Scope folder

↓

Plan folder

↓

Action folder

↓

Review folder

↓

Mission End folder

Once an unknown change issue has been examined in broad detail in the *Context* folder, the next stage is to explore or resolve in greater detail certain parts of the issue.
Each part has its own *Scope* folder which is used with *Scope* folder tool-sheets to choose the most effective option to resolve or explore one part of the issue. So there can be **many** *Scope* folders in one mission.
The basic *Scope* tool-sheets do this with two tool-sheets which look at a few main areas:
Tool-sheet 1 gives a generic set of options to explore or resolve most types of issues. Each option chosen will become a project.
Tool-sheet 2 looks at each project and asks for some basic setup information such as what it will do and who is involved. On the basic tool-sheet four projects can be described, the last is faded to suggest that more than four projects can be done.

How to use the tool-sheets
General instructions
These tool-sheets are designed to be used by a small team of 4-12 **Explorers*** to capture ideas, information and insights during a mission. A **Pathfinder** will make sure the Explorers stay on the task, while allowing unexpected insights to occur. An **Observer** will note down all the teams findings on the tool-sheets and additional paper if required.
Each tool-sheet has a general information section which is used to identify the issue, mission and the tool-sheet itself. The basic *Scope* tool-sheets are made up of a set of two tool-sheets. It is recommended to fill out them both to explore different options rather than the most obvious.
Each section of the tool-sheet with circles asks the team to explore options to explore or resolve gaps in the teams understanding of the issue.
The circles are not meant to be answered in any order, but rather start conversations.
The questions in the circles are not meant to cover every possible question, but rather the team can add their own context specific questions to the generic questions.
At the end of the basic *Scope* tool-sheets a selection of projects should be ready for the team to explore or resolve part of the issue. **Each project** will need planning, which is done by having its **own** *Plan* folder.
*See page 12 about the roles in Change-mapping.

Scope basic tool-sheet 1 of 2 — CHANGE-MAPPING

General information

Mission identification:
Shinrin/0001/2.2.22/new exhibition stand enquiry
Sheet identification:
Shinrin/0001/2.2.22/new exhibition stand enquiry, Scope basic tool-sheet 1
The issue is:
Marketing manager believes we should invest in a new exhibition stand.
Our mission is:
To confirm to the board that we should invest in a new exhibition stand.
This Scope folder explores or resolves which part of the issue?
Look at what our competitors are doing to promote their products.

What options are there to explore or resolve this part of the issue?

This seems a quick and simple option.
Search on the internet.
This seems a quick and simple option.

Search our old records.

Not sure if Library would have such detailed and up to date information.
Library search.

Visit a trade-show/conference.
Would be too late.

Interview stakeholders.
Not sure if this would give enough information, unless one knows more than us?

Interview experts.
Maybe we can talk to one of our friendly competitors?

Perform a small survey.
We could do this, but would need question list.

Use a more detailed tool-sheet.
This could be useful when setting the questions.

Perform a small scale test.
Not needed at this stage.

Concept Design.
When we are show what we are designing then we will need to do this.

Build a prototype.
When we are designing then we will need to do this.

Build a production version.
When we are show what we are designing then we will need to do this.

Do a large scale test.
If we did a website this could be useful.

Perform a large survey.
This could be useful asking what our clients want.

List the chosen options which will become projects.

Check what was found in the Context folder to guide decisions here!

Project 1
Each option will need a Plan folder
Use internet to find out what our competitors are doing.

Project 2
Each option will need a Plan folder
Setup a meeting with Beta company for information.

Project 3
Each option will need a Plan folder

Pro...
Each...
need a Pl...

Look through previous tool-sheets for guidance about standards, regulations and laws that might affect how we perform our options.

Scope basic tool-sheet 1 of 2 — CHANGE-MAPPING

General information

Mission identification:
Sheet identification:
The issue is:
Our mission is:
This Scope folder explores or resolves which part of the issue?

What options are there to explore or resolve this part of the issue?

Search on the internet.
Search our old records.
Library search.
Visit a trade-show/conference.

Interview a stakeholder.
Interview an expert.
Perform a small survey.

Use a more detailed tool-sheet.
Perform a small scale test.
Concept Design.
Build a prototype.

Build a production version.
Do a large scale test.
Perform a large survey.

List the chosen options which will become projects.

Check what was found in the Context folder to guide decisions here!

Project 1
Each option will need a Plan folder

Project 2
Each option will need a Plan folder

Project 3
Each option will need a Plan folder

Pro...
Each...
need a Pl...

Scope basic tool-sheet 2 of 2 — CHANGE-MAPPING

General information

Mission identification:
Shinrin/0001/2.2.22/new exhibition stand enquiry
Sheet identification:
Shinrin/0001/2.2.22/new exhibition stand enquiry, Scope basic tool-sheet 2
The issue is:
Marketing manager believes we should invest in a new exhibition stand.
Our mission is:
To confirm to the board that we should invest in a new exhibition stand.
This Scope folder explores or resolves which part of the issue?
Look at what our competitors are doing to promote their products.

Details about each project...

Project	*Use internet to find out what our competitors are doing with exhibition stands.*	*Setup a meeting with Beta company for a bit of advice about exhibition stands.*
Project order	First	Second
Project manager	Alpha team leader	Bravo team leader
Project team	Alpha team	Bravo team leader
Estimated start/finish	Four hours	One hour
Estimated budget	Apart from time no extra costs	Apart from time no extra costs

---

Scope basic tool-sheet 2 of 2 — CHANGE-MAPPING

General information

Mission identification:
Sheet identification:
The issue is:
Our mission is:
This Scope folder explores or resolves which part of the issue?

Details about each project...

| Project |
| Project order |
| Project manager |
| Project team |
| Estimated start/finish |
| Estimated budget |

To show how the tool-sheets are used on the left one is filled in with a worked example.
On the right is a blank version which can be photocopied for your own projects.

Scope basic tool-sheet 1 of 2

CHANGE▸MAPPING
CONNECTING BUSINESS TOOLS TO MANAGE CHANGE

General information

Mission identification:
Shirnrin/0001/2.2.22/new exhibition stand enquiry
Sheet identification:
Shirnrin/0001/2.2.22/new exhibition stand enquiry, Scope basic tool-sheet 1
The issue is:
Marketing manager believes we should invest in a new exhibition stand.
Our mission is:
To confirm to the board whether we should invest in a new exhibition stand.
This *Scope* folder explores or resolves which part of the issue?
Look at what our competitors are doing to promote their products.

What options are there to explore or resolve this part of the issue?

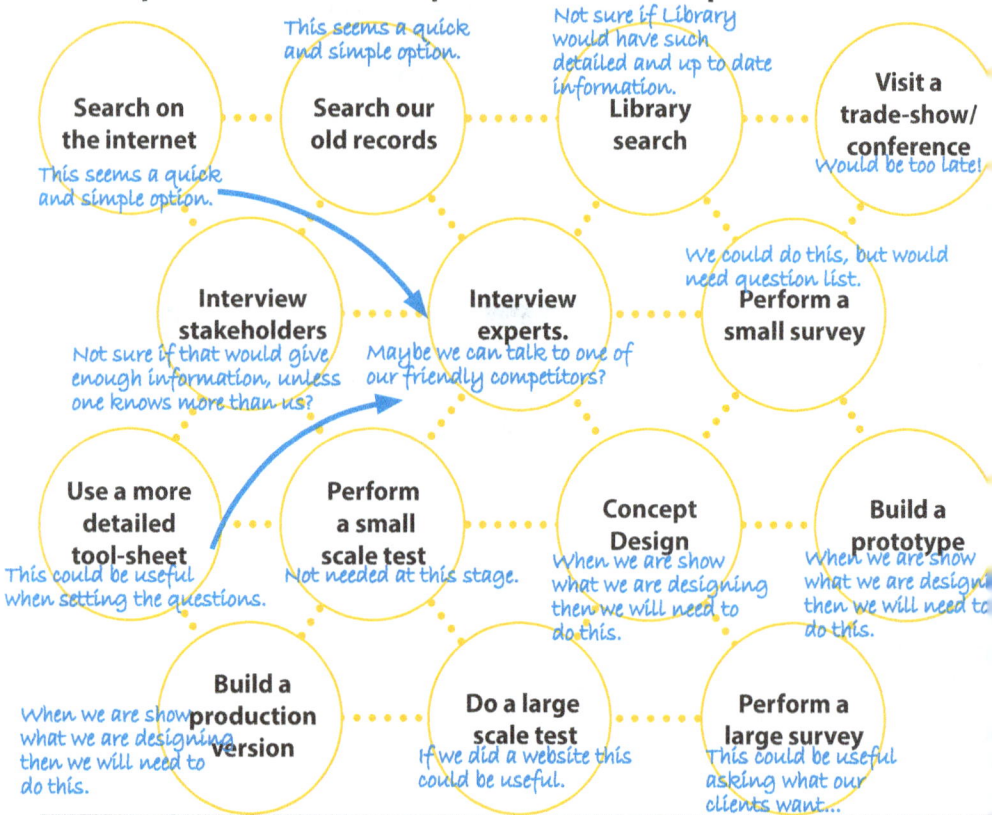

Search on the internet

This seems a quick and simple option.

Search our old records

Not sure if Library would have such detailed and up to date information.

Library search

Visit a trade-show/ conference

Would be too late!

This seems a quick and simple option.

Interview stakeholders

Not sure if that would give enough information, unless one knows more than us?

Interview experts

Maybe we can talk to one of our friendly competitors?

We could do this, but would need question list.

Perform a small survey

Use a more detailed tool-sheet

This could be useful when setting the questions.

Perform a small scale test

Not needed at this stage.

Concept Design

When we are show what we are designing then we will need to do this.

Build a prototype

When we are show what we are designing then we will need to do this.

When we are show what we are designing then we will need to do this.

Build a production version

Do a large scale test

If we did a website this could be useful.

Perform a large survey

This could be useful asking what our clients want...

List the chosen options which will become projects.

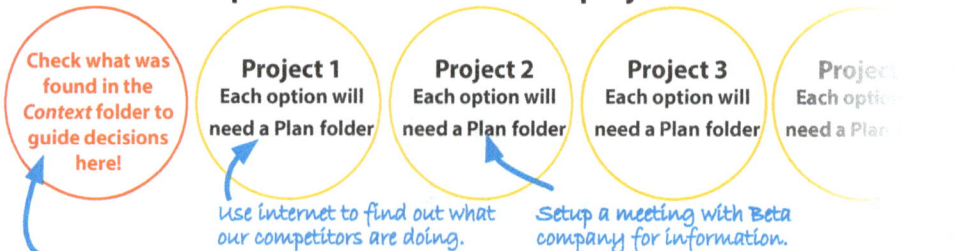

Check what was found in the *Context* folder to guide decisions here!

Project 1
Each option will need a Plan folder

Project 2
Each option will need a Plan folder

Project 3
Each option will need a Plan folder

Proje...
Each optio... need a Pla...

Use internet to find out what our competitors are doing.

Setup a meeting with Beta company for information.

Look through previous tool-sheets for guidance about standards, regulations and laws that might affect how we perform our options.

CHANGE→MAPPING
CONNECTING BUSINESS TOOLS TO MANAGE CHANGE

General information

Mission identification:

Sheet identification:

The issue is:

Our mission is:

This *Scope* folder explores or resolves which part of the issue?

What options are there to explore or resolve this part of the issue?

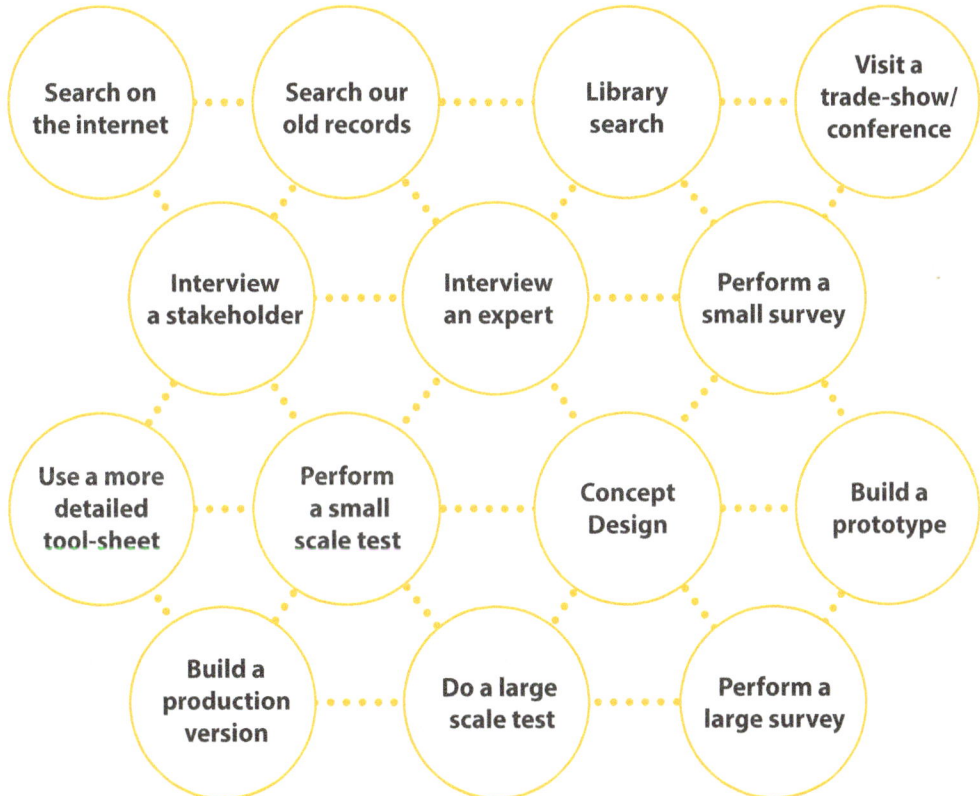

Search on the internet

Search our old records

Library search

Visit a trade-show/ conference

Interview a stakeholder

Interview an expert

Perform a small survey

Use a more detailed tool-sheet

Perform a small scale test

Concept Design

Build a prototype

Build a production version

Do a large scale test

Perform a large survey

List the chosen options which will become projects.

Check what was found in the *Context* folder to guide decisions here!

Project 1
Each option will need a Plan folder

Project 2
Each option will need a Plan folder

Project 3
Each option will need a Plan folder

Proje...
Each opt...
need a Pla...

Scope basic tool-sheet 2 of 2

CHANGE→MAPPING
CONNECTING BUSINESS TOOLS TO MANAGE CHANGE

General information

Mission identification:
Shirnrin/0001/2.2.22/new exhibition stand enquiry
Sheet identification:
Shirnrin/0001/2.2.22/new exhibition stand enquiry, Scope basic tool-sheet 2
The issue is:
Marketing manager believes we should invest in a new exhibition stand.
Our mission is:
To confirm to the board whether we should invest in a new exhibition stand.
This *Scope* folder explores or resolves which part of the issue?
Look at what our competitors are doing to promote their products.

Details about each project...

Project	Use internet to find out what our competitors are doing with exhibition stands.	Setup a meeting with Beta company for a bit of advice about exhibition stands.		
Project order	First	Second		
Project manager	Alpha team leader	Bravo team leader		
Project team	Alpha team	Bravo team leader		
Estimated start/finish	Four hours	One hour		
Estimated budget	Apart from time no extra costs	Apart from time no extra costs		

CHANGE→MAPPING
CONNECTING BUSINESS TOOLS TO MANAGE CHANGE

General information

Mission identification:

Sheet identification:

The issue is:

Our mission is:

This *Scope* folder explores or resolves which part of the issue?

Details about each project...

Project

Project order

Project manager

Project team

Estimated start/finish

Estimated budget

Chapter 8: The *Plan* tool-sheets
Planning how to explore or resolve part of the issue

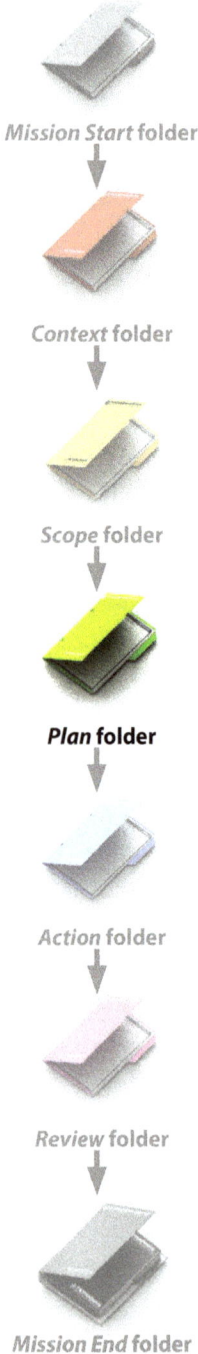

CHANGE→MAPPING
CONNECTING BUSINESS TOOLS TO MANAGE CHANGE

Mission Start folder

Context folder

Scope folder

Plan folder

Action folder

Review folder

Mission End folder

The *Plan* folder tool-sheets are used to plan how projects, chosen in the *Scope* folder, will actually work.

The basic *Plan* tool-sheets do this with two tool-sheets which look at a few main areas:

Tool-sheet 1 makes sure that everything is in place before the plan is enacted, such as: are the right skills and information available before the action starts?

In addition how can problems be avoided before they happen such as going over budget or having faulty equipment.

Tool-sheet 2 breaks down each project into specific tasks and asks which order they should happen and when they may finish for example. In the basic tool-sheet there is space only for a few tasks, with the lines fading at the bottom to suggest that in a real project more space may be required. This will be used in the *Action* folder, one filled in and one blank copy.

How to use the tool-sheets
General instructions
These tool-sheets are designed to be used by a small team of 4-12 **Explorers*** to capture ideas, information and insights during a mission. A **Pathfinder** will make sure the Explorers stay on the task, while allowing unexpected insights to occur. An **Observer** will note down all the teams findings on the tool-sheets and additional paper if required.

Each tool-sheet has a general information section which is used to identify the issue, mission and the tool-sheet itself. The basic *Plan* tool-sheets are made up of a set of two tool-sheets. It is recommended to fill out them both to obtain a broad view of the plan and any potential problems that might occur, before enacting the plan.

Each section of the tool-sheet with circles asks the team to produce plans to explore or resolve on part of an issue, in detail. The circles are not meant to be answered in any order, but rather start conversations.

The questions in the circles are not meant to cover every possible question, but rather the team will add their own context specific questions to the generic questions.

At the end of the basic *Plan* tool-sheets a workable plan should be ready for a team to use to explore or resolve a specific part of the issue.

This plan will be enacted in the *Action* folder.

*See page 12 about the roles in Change-mapping.

Plan basic tool-sheet 1 of 2   ⓘ CHANGE•MAPPING

General information

Mission identification:
Shimrin/0001/2.2.22/new exhibition stand enquiry
Sheet identification:
Shimrin/0001/2.2.22/new exhibition stand enquiry, Plan basic tool-sheet 1
The issue is:
Marketing manager believes we should invest in a new exhibition stand.
Our mission is:
To confirm to the board that we should invest in a new exhibition stand.
This *Scope* folder explores or resolves which part of the issue?
Look at what our competitors are doing to promote their products.
This *Plan* tool-sheet is used to plan?
Setup a meeting with Beta company for information.

Are these in place before the plan is enacted?

The right skills and experience? *The task seems not too specialised.* · · · The right information? *We think so.* · · · The right information? *We could do this, but would need question list.* · · · The right budget? *The budget seems fine.*

The right people? *Bring in some of the marketing team* · · · The right equipment? *Laptop, wifi pen and paper.* · · · A back-up plan? *No, but we have sufficient time to explore other options.*

Enough time? *It should be sufficient time.* · · · The right location? *Our offices.* · · · A way to record the action taking place! *Will take notes to note how process went.* → This will needed in the *Review* folder!

How might these be avoided when enacting the plan?

The wrong skills and experience! *If the expert doesn't have any useful information, it would be a waste of time.* · · · The wrong materials! *Don't think this should be an issue.* · · · No information! *Our questions need to be prepared, otherwise a waste of time.* · · · Over budget! *If the meeting went on too long, or too large a food!*

Weather issues! *If not in our offices, weather affect things.* · · · The equipment doesn't work! *If we were not in offices then we need batteries.* · · · No back-up plan! *If the meeting is not planning we will slow down, wait a ½ hour.*

Not enough time! *It should be sufficient time.* · · · The wrong location! *Maybe a more neutral location?* · · · Arguments! *Hopefully this shouldn't occur as informal meeting.* · · · No leadership! *Have the meeting stays on target.*

Plan basic tool-sheet 2 of 2   ⓘ CHANGE•MAPPING

General information

Mission identification:
Shimrin/0001/2.2.22/new exhibition stand enquiry
Sheet identification:
Shimrin/0001/2.2.22/new exhibition stand enquiry, Plan basic tool-sheet 1
The issue is:
Marketing manager believes we should invest in a new exhibition stand.
Our mission is:
To confirm to the board that we should invest in a new exhibition stand.
This *Scope* folder explores or resolves which part of the issue?
Look at what our competitors are doing to promote their products.
This *Plan* tool-sheet is used to plan?
Setup a meeting with Beta company for information.

Check what was found in the *Context* folder to guide decisions here! *Look through previous tool-sheets for guidance about standards, regulations and laws that might affect how we perform our options.*

Post task will need its own Review folder, such as post meeting de-brief.

Reviewing of task will be done in the *Review* folder

Estimated task breakdown for project...

Task	People	Equipment and location	Skills and experience	Information	Materials	Start/Finish
Pre-meeting setup	Marketing team	Laptop, wifi and our office	Basic office skills	Our questions	Food, water and paper	Five minutes
Meeting start	Marketing team and expert	Laptop, wifi and our office	Basic office skills	Our questions	Food, water and paper	Five minutes
Meeting end	Marketing team and expert	Laptop, wifi and our office	Basic office skills	Experts answers	Food, water and paper	40 minutes
Post meeting	Marketing team	Notes form meeting	Basic office skills and Pathfinder, Observe	Experts answers	Food, water and paper Review tool-sheets	30 minutes

---

Plan basic tool-sheet 1 of 2   ⓘ CHANGE•MAPPING

General information

Mission identification:

Sheet identification:

The issue is:

Our mission is:

This *Scope* folder explores or resolves which part of the issue?

This *Plan* tool-sheet is used to plan?

Are these in place before the plan is enacted?

The right skills and experience? · · · The right materials? · · · · · The right information? · · · The right budget?

The right people? · · · · · The right equipment? · · · · · A back-up plan?

Enough time? · · · · The right location? · · · · A way to record the action taking place → This will needed in the *Review* folder!

How might these be avoided when enacting the plan?

The wrong skills and experience! · · · The wrong materials! · · · No information! · · · Over budget!

Weather issues! · · · · · The equipment doesn't work! · · · No back-up plan!

Not enough time! · · · · The wrong location! · · · · Arguments! · · · · No leadership!

Plan basic tool-sheet 2 of 2   ⓘ CHANGE•MAPPING

General information

Mission identification:

Sheet identification:

The issue is:

Our mission is:

This *Scope* folder explores or resolves which part of the issue?

This *Plan* tool-sheet is used to plan?

Check what was found in the *Context* folder to guide decisions here!

Reviewing of task will be done in the *Review* folder

Estimated task breakdown for project...

Task	People	Equipment and location	Skills and experience	Information	Materials	Start/Finish

To show how the tool-sheets are used on the left one is filled in with a worked example.
On the right is a blank version which can be photocopied for your own projects.

Plan basic tool-sheet 1 of 2

CHANGE→MAPPING
CONNECTING BUSINESS TOOLS TO MANAGE CHANGE

General information

Mission identification:
Shirmin/0001/2.2.22/new exhibition stand enquiry
Sheet identification:
Shirmin/0001/2.2.22/new exhibition stand enquiry, Plan basic tool-sheet 1
The issue is:
Marketing manager believes we should invest in a new exhibition stand.
Our mission is:
To confirm to the board whether we should invest in a new exhibition stand.
This *Scope* folder explores or resolves which part of the issue?
Look at what our competitors are doing to promote their products.
This *Plan* tool-sheet is used to plan?
Setup a meeting with Beta company for information.

Are these in place before the plan is enacted?

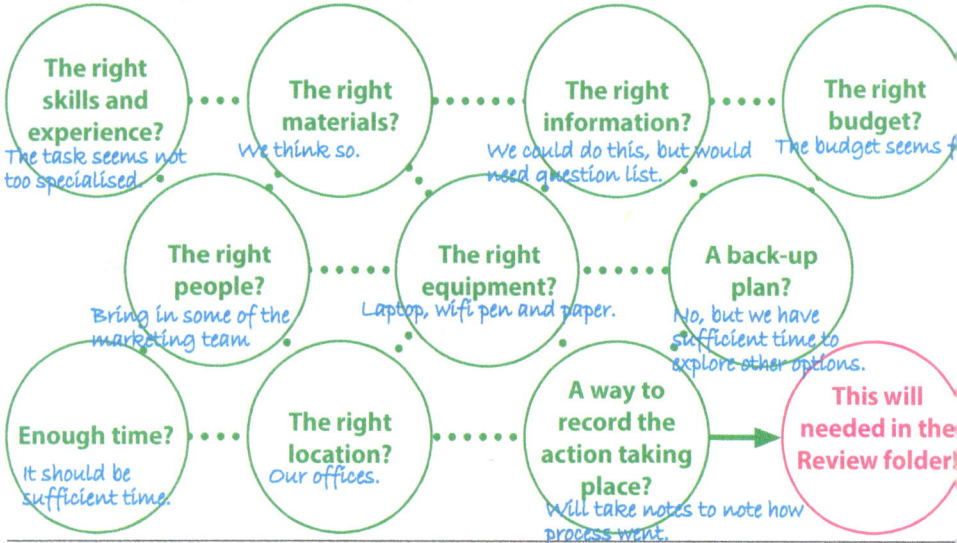

The right skills and experience?
The task seems not too specialised.

The right materials?
We think so.

The right information?
We could do this, but would need question list.

The right budget?
The budget seems f...

The right people?
Bring in some of the marketing team

The right equipment?
Laptop, wifi pen and paper.

A back-up plan?
No, but we have sufficient time to explore other options.

Enough time?
It should be sufficient time.

The right location?
Our offices.

A way to record the action taking place?
Will take notes to note how process went.

This will needed in the Review folder!

How might these be avoided when enacting the plan?

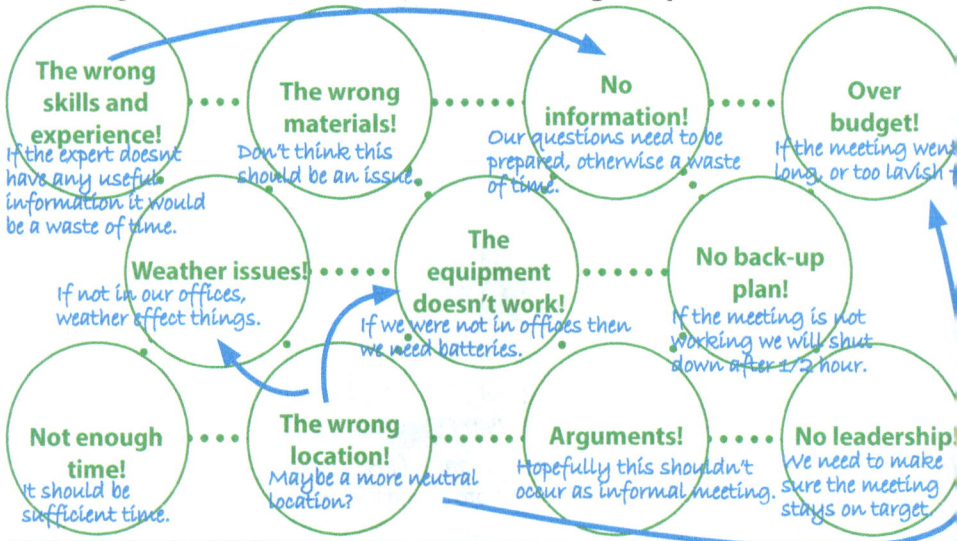

The wrong skills and experience!
If the expert doesn't have any useful information it would be a waste of time.

The wrong materials!
Don't think this should be an issue.

No information!
Our questions need to be prepared, otherwise a waste of time.

Over budget!
If the meeting went long, or too lavish t...

Weather issues!
If not in our offices, weather effect things.

The equipment doesn't work!
If we were not in offices then we need batteries.

No back-up plan!
If the meeting is not working we will shut down after 1/2 hour.

Not enough time!
It should be sufficient time.

The wrong location!
Maybe a more neutral location?

Arguments!
Hopefully this shouldn't occur as informal meeting.

No leadership!
We need to make sure the meeting stays on target.

Plan basic tool-sheet 1 of 2

CHANGE→MAPPING
CONNECTING BUSINESS TOOLS TO MANAGE CHANGE

General information

Mission identification:

Sheet identification:

The issue is:

Our mission is:

This *Scope* folder explores or resolves which part of the issue?

This *Plan* tool-sheet is used to plan?

Are these in place before the plan is enacted?

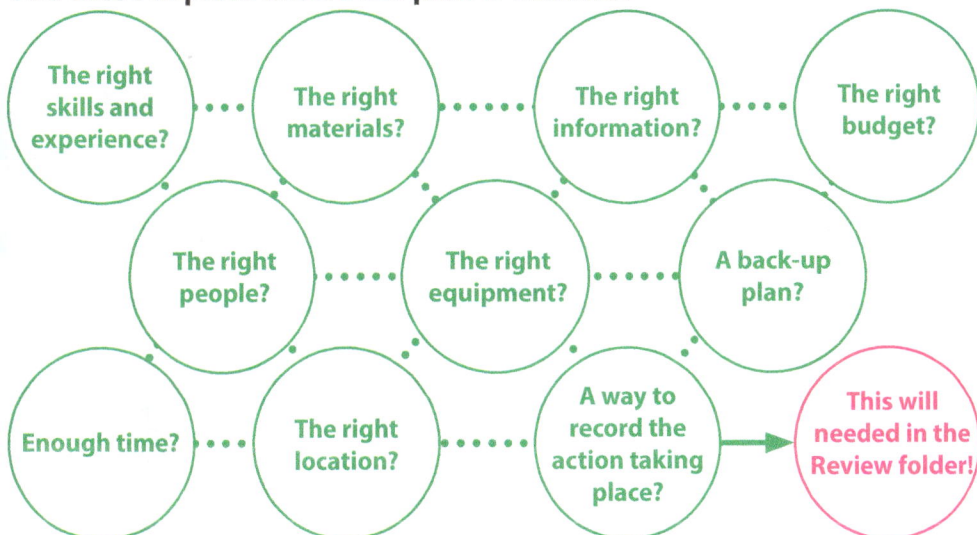

The right skills and experience?

The right materials?

The right information?

The right budget?

The right people?

The right equipment?

A back-up plan?

Enough time?

The right location?

A way to record the action taking place?

This will needed in the Review folder!

How might these be avoided when enacting the plan?

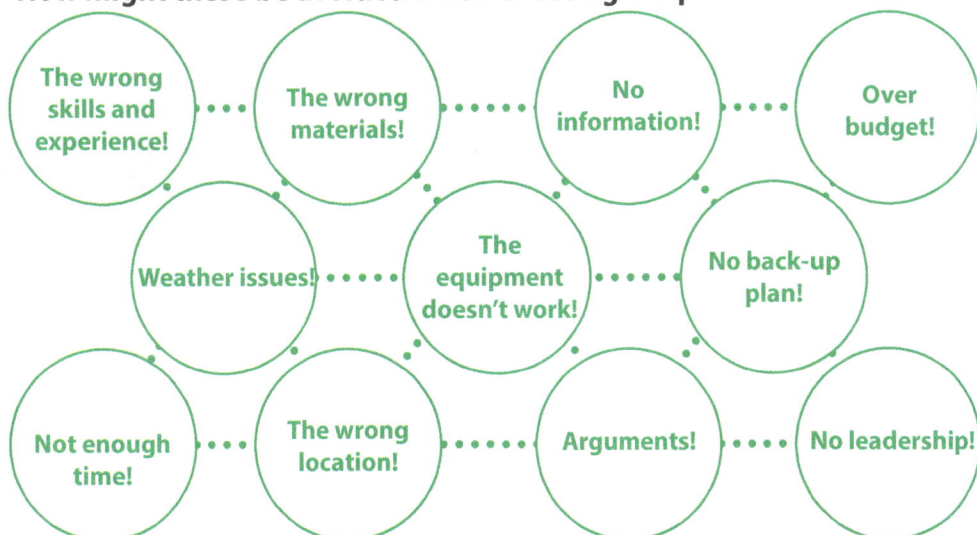

The wrong skills and experience!

The wrong materials!

No information!

Over budget!

Weather issues!

The equipment doesn't work!

No back-up plan!

Not enough time!

The wrong location!

Arguments!

No leadership!

Plan basic tool-sheet 2 of 2

CHANGE→MAPPING
CONNECTING BUSINESS TOOLS TO MANAGE CHANGE

General information

Mission identification:
Shirnrin/0001/2.2.22/new exhibition stand enquiry
Sheet identification:
Shirnrin/0001/2.2.22/new exhibition stand enquiry, Plan basic tool-sheet 1
The issue is:
Marketing manager believes we should invest in a new exhibition stand.
Our mission is:
To confirm to the board whether we should invest in a new exhibition stand.
This *Scope* folder explores or resolves which part of the issue?
Look at what our competitors are doing to promote their products.
This *Plan* tool-sheet is used to plan?
Setup a meeting with Beta company for information.

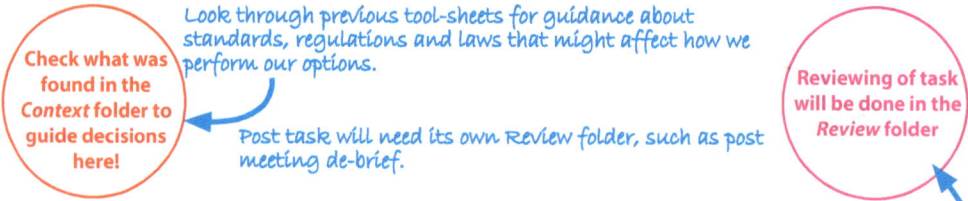

Check what was found in the *Context* folder to guide decisions here!

Look through previous tool-sheets for guidance about standards, regulations and laws that might affect how we perform our options.

Post task will need its own *Review* folder, such as post meeting de-brief.

Reviewing of task will be done in the *Review* folder

Estimated task breakdown for project...

Task	People	Equipment and location	Skills and experience	Information	Materials	Start/Finish
Pre-meeting setup	Marketing team	Laptop, wifi and our office	Basic office skills	Our questions	Food, water and paper	Five minutes
Meeting start	Marketing team and expert	Laptop, wifi and our office	Basic office skills	Our questions	Food, water and paper	Five minutes
Meeting end	Marketing team and expert	Laptop, wifi and our office	Basic office skills	Experts answers	Food, water and paper	40 minutes
Post meeting	Marketing team	Notes form meeting	Basic office skills and Pathfinder, Observer	Experts answers	Food, water and paper Review tool-sheets	30 minutes

CHANGE→MAPPING
CONNECTING BUSINESS TOOLS TO MANAGE CHANGE

General information

Mission identification:

Sheet identification:

The issue is:

Our mission is:

This *Scope* folder explores or resolves which part of the issue?

This *Plan* tool-sheet is used to plan?

Check what was found in the *Context* folder to guide decisions here!

Reviewing of task will be done in the *Review* folder

Estimated task breakdown for project...

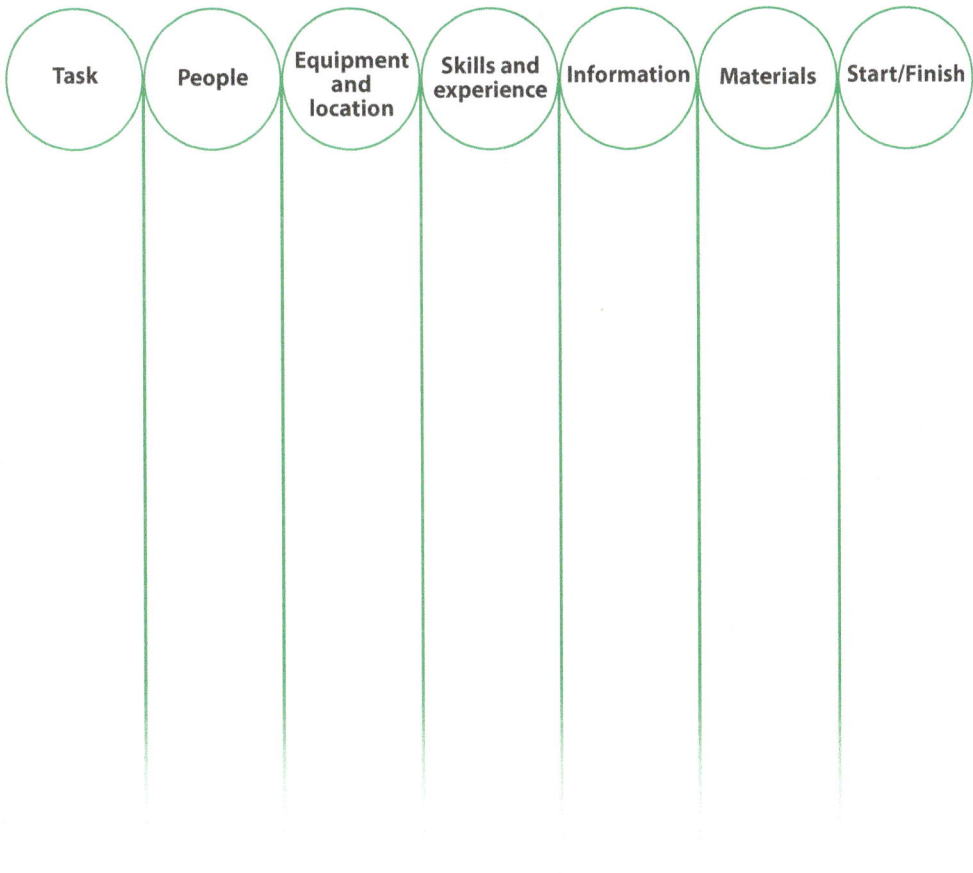

Task	People	Equipment and location	Skills and experience	Information	Materials	Start/Finish

Chapter 9: Tool-sheets in the *Action* folder
Pre-flight checklists and documenting what happened

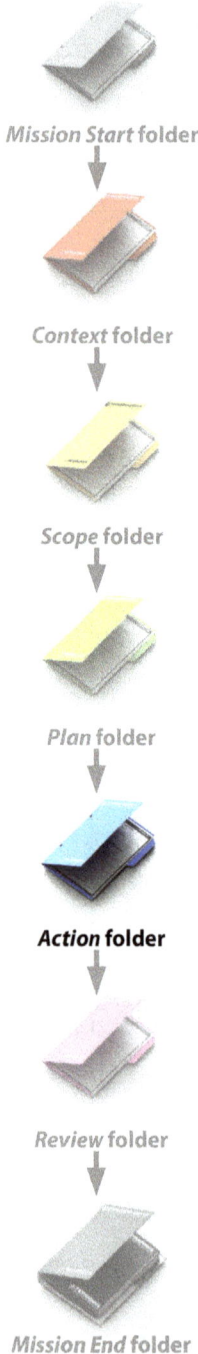

CHANGE→MAPPING
CONNECTING BUSINESS TOOLS TO MANAGE CHANGE

Mission Start folder

Context folder

Scope folder

Plan folder

Action* folder

Review folder

Mission End folder

The *Action* folder works slightly differently to the other folders in *Change-mapping*. In the other folders, questions are posed to a team about **how** they will explore or resolve part of the issue. In this folder part of the issue **is** being explored or resolved. So tool-sheets from other folders, especially the *Plan* folder, are used as pre-flight checklists and to **record** the enactment of the plan taking place.

For example if a meeting had been planned in the *Plan* folder, in the *Action* folder the *Plan* tool-sheets would be used to check that everything needed for the meeting was there. ***Those tool-sheets would also be used to record how the meeting was run and what information was found.***

This information will then be used to review how the action went in the next folder, the *Review* folder.

How to use the tool-sheets
General instructions
A **pre-filled** in set of *Plan* tool-sheets will be needed. You should have done these previously in the *Plan* folder. These will act as a pre-flight checklist.

A **blank** set of the *Plan* tool-sheets will be needed as the **Observer*** will write down what happens at each stage of the enactment of the plan.

You may also need to capture any information, for example an interviewee's answers in an interview or test results.

This information will then be refered to in the next folder, the *Review* folder. There what happened will be compared to what was meant to happen and the notes from the *Action* folder will be required as evidence.

*See page 12 about the roles in Change-mapping.

Plan basic tool-sheet 1 of 2

⊙ CHANGE-MAPPING

General information

Mission identification:
Shimrin/0001/2.2.22/new exhibition stand enquiry
Sheet identification:
Shimrin/0001/2.2.22/new exhibition stand enquiry, Plan basic tool-sheet 1
The issue is:
Marketing manager believes we should invest in a new exhibition stand.
Our mission is:
To confirm to the board that we should invest in a new exhibition stand.
This Scope folder explores or resolves which part of the issue?
Look at what our competitors are doing to promote their products.
This Plan tool-sheet is used to plan?
Setup a meeting with Beta company for information.

Are these in place before the plan is enacted?

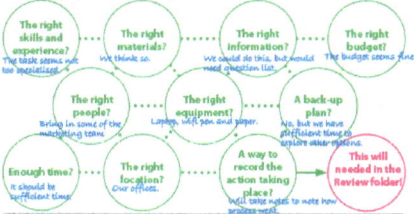

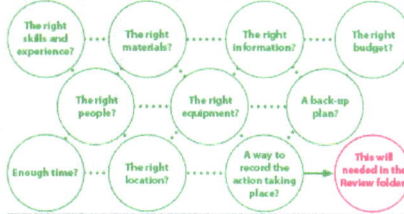

The right skills and experience? The task seems not too specialized.
The right materials? We think so.
The right information? We could do this, but would need question list.
The right budget? The budget seems fine.

The right people? Bring in some of the marketing team.
The right equipment? Laptop, wifi, pen and paper.
A back-up plan? No, but we have sufficient time to explore other options.

Enough time? It should be sufficient time.
The right location? Our office.
A way to record the action taking place? Will take notes to note how process went.
This will needed in the Review folder!

How might these be avoided when enacting the plan?

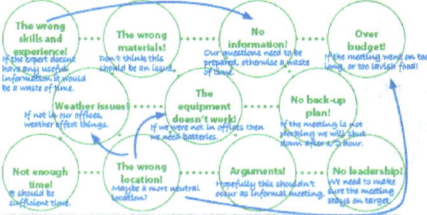

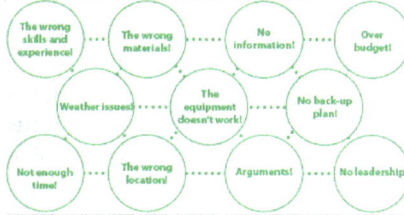

The wrong skills and experience! If the expert doesn't have any useful information it would be a waste of time.
The wrong materials! Don't think this should be an issue.
No information! Our questions need to be prepared, otherwise a waste of time.
Over budget! If the meeting went on too long, or too lavish food!

Weather issues! If not in our office, weather affect things.
The equipment doesn't work! If we were not in offices then we need batteries.
No back-up plan! If the meeting is not planning we will slow down over a ½ hour.

Not enough time! It should be sufficient time.
The wrong location! Maybe a more neutral location?
Arguments! Hopefully this shouldn't occur as informal meeting.
No leadership! We need to make sure the meeting stays on target.

Plan basic tool-sheet 1 of 2

⊙ CHANGE-MAPPING

General information

Mission identification:

Sheet identification:

The issue is:

Our mission is:

This Scope folder explores or resolves which part of the issue?

This Plan tool-sheet is used to plan?

Are these in place before the plan is enacted?

The right skills and experience?
The right materials?
The right information?
The right budget?

The right people?
The right equipment?
A back-up plan?

Enough time?
The right location?
A way to record the action taking place?
This will needed in the Review folder!

How might these be avoided when enacting the plan?

The wrong skills and experience!
The wrong materials!
No information!
Over budget!

Weather issues!
The equipment doesn't work!
No back-up plan!

Not enough time!
The wrong location!
Arguments!
No leadership!

Plan basic tool-sheet 2 of 2

⊙ CHANGE-MAPPING

General information

Mission identification:
Shimrin/0001/2.2.22/new exhibition stand enquiry
Sheet identification:
Shimrin/0001/2.2.22/new exhibition stand enquiry, Plan basic tool-sheet 2
The issue is:
Marketing manager believes we should invest in a new exhibition stand.
Our mission is:
To confirm to the board that we should invest in a new exhibition stand.
This Scope folder explores or resolves which part of the issue?
Look at what our competitors are doing to promote their products.
This Plan tool-sheet is used to plan?
Setup a meeting with Beta company for information.

Check what was found in the Context folder to guide decisions here!
Look through previous tool-sheets for guidance about standards, regulations and laws that might affect how we perform our options.
Post task will need its own Review folder, such as post meeting de-brief.
Reviewing of task will be done in the Review folder

Estimated task breakdown for project...

Task	People	Equipment and location	Skills and experience	Information	Materials	Start/Finish
Pre-meeting setup	Marketing team	Laptop, wifi and our office	Basic office skills	Our questions	Food, water and paper	Five minutes
Meeting start	Marketing team and expert	Laptop, wifi and our office	Basic office skills	Our questions	Food, water and paper	Five minutes
Meeting end	Marketing team and expert	Laptop, wifi and our office	Basic office skills	Experts answers	Food, water and paper	40 minutes
Post meeting	Marketing team	Notes form meeting	Basic office skills and Pathfinder, Observer	Experts answers	Food, water and paper review tool-sheets	30 minutes

---

Plan basic tool-sheet 2 of 2

⊙ CHANGE-MAPPING

General information

Mission identification:

Sheet identification:

The issue is:

Our mission is:

This Scope folder explores or resolves which part of the issue?

This Plan tool-sheet is used to plan?

Check what was found in the Context folder to guide decisions here!
Reviewing of task will be done in the Review folder

Estimated task breakdown for project...

Task	People	Equipment and location	Skills and experience	Information	Materials	Start/Finish

---

The tool-sheets, from the Plan folder are used in the Action folder as pre-flight checklists and to record how the action went and what was found.

Chapter 10: The *Review* tool-sheet
Reviewing the exploration or resolution of one part of the issue

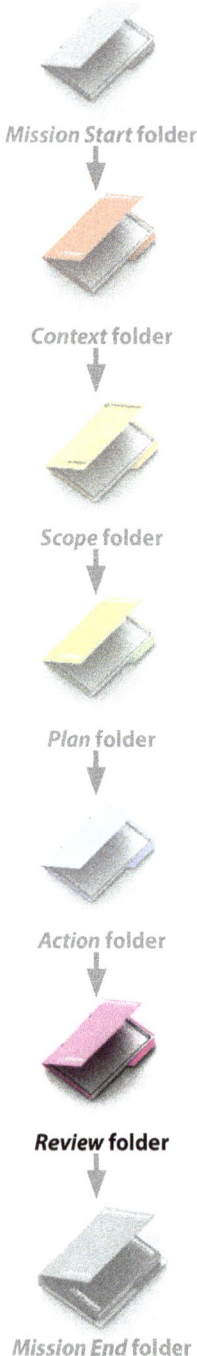

CHANGE→MAPPING
CONNECTING BUSINESS TOOLS TO MANAGE CHANGE

Mission Start folder

↓

Context folder

↓

Scope folder

↓

Plan folder

↓

Action folder

↓

Review folder

↓

Mission End folder

Every plan and its enactment should have its own review, which is done in the *Review* folder with a basic *Review* tool-sheet.

In order to perform a review other tool-sheets from the mission will be required, especially the record of the action. The tool-sheet asks how the enactment of the plan differed from what was planned to happen. In addition the outcome of the enactment is questioned, was it successful, were there unexpected events and so on.

Once this tool-sheet has been completed then any other outstanding parts of the mission need to be completed before moving to the last folder, the *Mission End* folder.

There instead of *parts* of the mission being reviewed, *all* of the mission is reviewed.

How to use the tool-sheet
General instructions

This tool-sheet is designed to be used by a small team of 4-12 **Explorers*** to capture ideas, information and insights during a mission. A **Pathfinder** will make sure the Explorers stay on the task, while allowing unexpected insights to occur.

An **Observer** will note down all the teams findings on the tool-sheet and additional paper if required.

The tool-sheet has a general information section which is used to identify the issue, mission and the tool-sheet itself. It is recommended to review what happened during the *Action* folder and to see what can be learnt.

Each section of the tool-sheet with circles asks the team to review the exploration or resolution of part of the issue. The circles are not meant to be answered in any order, but rather start conversations.

The questions in the circles are not meant to cover every possible question, but rather the team can add their own context specific questions to the generic questions.

Once the review has been completed, complete any other outstanding parts of the mission before going to the last part of the mission, the *Mission End* folder.

*See page 12 about the roles in Change-mapping.

Review basic tool-sheet — CHANGE-MAPPING

General information

Mission identification:
Shimrin/0001/2.2.22/new exhibition stand enquiry
Sheet identification:
Shimrin/0001/2.2.22/new exhibition stand enquiry. Review basic tool-sheet
The issue is:
Marketing manager believes we should invest in a new exhibition stand.
Our mission is:
To confirm to the board that we should invest in a new exhibition stand.
The Scope folder explored or resolved which part of the issue?
Look at what our competitors are doing to promote their products.
The accompanying Plan tool-sheet was used to plan?
Setup a meeting with Beta company for information.

How did the enactment of the task differ from the plan? Was there...

- The right skills and experience? *we think yes*
- The right materials? *we think so.*
- The right information? *Our questions were a little vague.*
- The right budget? *The budget was good.*
- The right people? *Might have been good to bring in people from different depts.*
- The right equipment? *Yes.*
- A back-up plan? *Yes. But not needed.*
- Enough time? *We could have done with another hour for this meeting.*
- The right location? *The expert seemed relaxed at our offices.*
- A way to record the action taking place? *The Observer recorded how the meeting was conducted.*
- Check what was found in the Context folder when reviewing!

What was the outcome of the task enactment?

- What was learnt by doing the task? *Our competitors uses exhibition stands for shows across the world. They seem to bring in a lot of enquiries afterwards. Her thought one was a good investment.*
- Was the task successful? *We felt it was as we now understand what one of our competitors does regarding exhibition stands.*
- Were there unexpected events or findings? *We had assumed the expert would only talk about exhibition stands but he had some interesting ideas about social media and printed brochures.*
- If the task was repeated, what could be improved? *We would be better prepared with questions for the meeting.*
- Check what was found in the Context folder when reviewing! *We will check the Context folder tool-sheets when performing the review of the task enactment.*

Review basic tool-sheet — CHANGE-MAPPING

General information

Mission identification:
Sheet identification:
The issue is:
Our mission is:
The Scope folder explored or resolved which part of the issue?
The accompanying Plan tool-sheet was used to plan?

How did the enactment of the task differ from the plan? Was there...

- The right skills and experience?
- The right materials?
- The right information?
- The right budget?
- The right people?
- The right equipment?
- A back-up plan?
- Enough time?
- The right location?
- A way to record the action taking place?
- Check what was found in the Context folder when reviewing!

What was the outcome of the task enactment?

- What was learnt by doing the task?
- Was the task successful?
- Were there unexpected events or findings?
- If the task was repeated, what could be improved?
- Check what was found in the Context folder when reviewing!

To show how the tool-sheets are used on the left one is filled in with a worked example. On the right is a blank version which can be photocopied for your own projects.

Note: To effectively use the Review tool-sheet filled-in copies of the Context, Scope, Plan and Action record will be required.

Review basic tool-sheet

CHANGE→MAPPING
CONNECTING BUSINESS TOOLS TO MANAGE CHANGE

General information

Mission identification:
Shirnrin/0001/2.2.22/new exhibition stand enquiry
Sheet identification:
Shirnrin/0001/2.2.22/new exhibition stand enquiry, Review basic tool-sheet
The issue is:
Marketing manager believes we should invest in a new exhibition stand.
Our mission is:
To confirm to the board whether we should invest in a new exhibition stand.
The *Scope* folder explored or resolved which part of the issue?
Look at what our competitors are doing to promote their products.
The accompanying *Plan* tool-sheet was used to plan?
Setup a meeting with Beta company for information.

How did the enactment of the task differ from the plan? Was there...

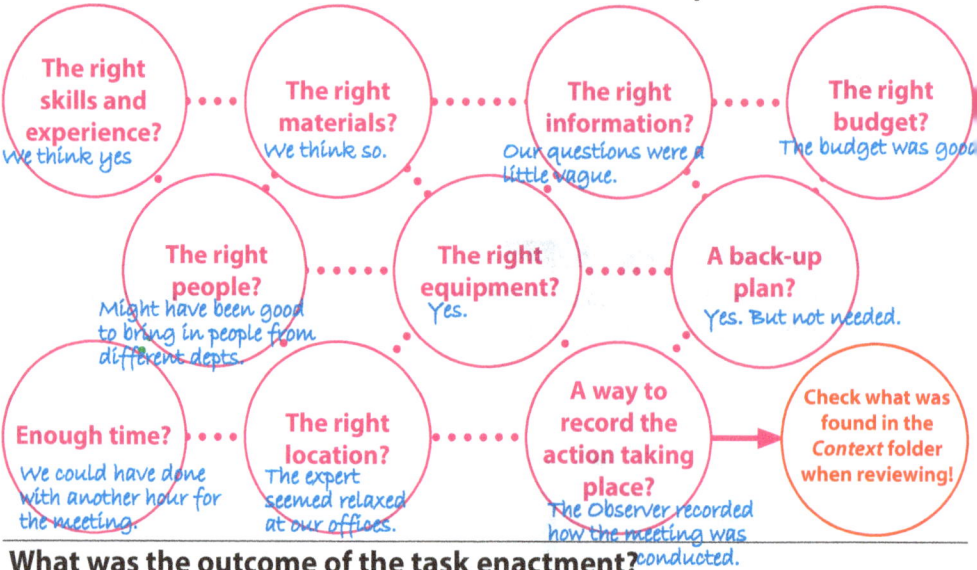

The right skills and experience?
We think yes

The right materials?
We think so.

The right information?
Our questions were a little vague.

The right budget?
The budget was good

The right people?
Might have been good to bring in people from different depts.

The right equipment?
Yes.

A back-up plan?
Yes. But not needed.

Enough time?
We could have done with another hour for the meeting.

The right location?
The expert seemed relaxed at our offices.

A way to record the action taking place?
The Observer recorded how the meeting was conducted.

Check what was found in the *Context* folder when reviewing!

What was the outcome of the task enactment?

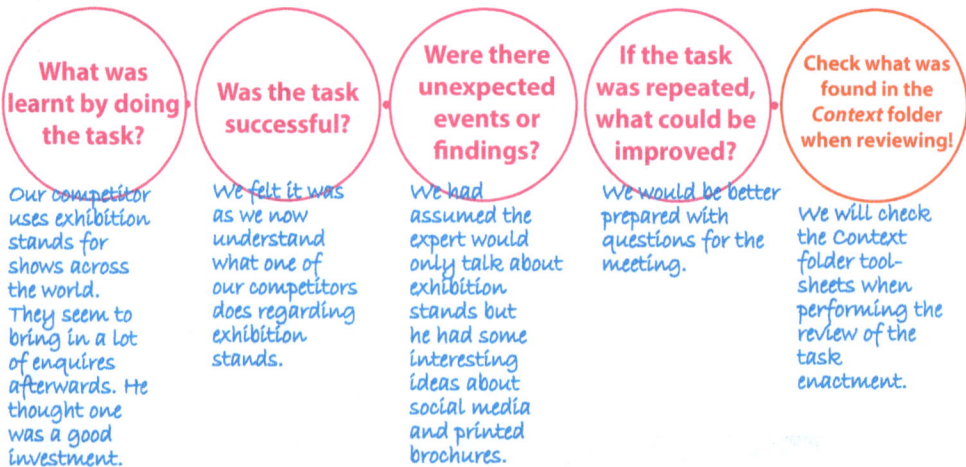

What was learnt by doing the task?
Our competitor uses exhibition stands for shows across the world. They seem to bring in a lot of enquires afterwards. He thought one was a good investment.

Was the task successful?
We felt it was as we now understand what one of our competitors does regarding exhibition stands.

Were there unexpected events or findings?
We had assumed the expert would only talk about exhibition stands but he had some interesting ideas about social media and printed brochures.

If the task was repeated, what could be improved?
We would be better prepared with questions for the meeting.

Check what was found in the *Context* folder when reviewing!
We will check the Context folder tool-sheets when performing the review of the task enactment.

Review basic tool-sheet

General information

Mission identification:

Sheet identification:

The issue is:

Our mission is:

The *Scope* folder explored or resolved which part of the issue?

The accompanying *Plan* tool-sheet was used to plan?

How did the enactment of the task differ from the plan? Was there...

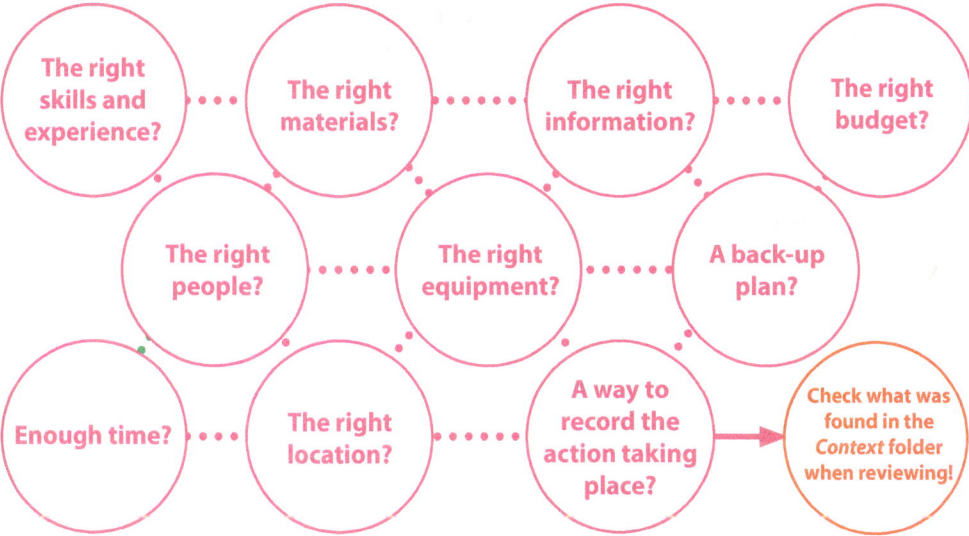

The right skills and experience?

The right materials?

The right information?

The right budget?

The right people?

The right equipment?

A back-up plan?

Enough time?

The right location?

A way to record the action taking place?

Check what was found in the *Context* folder when reviewing!

What was the outcome of the task enactment?

What was learnt by doing the task?

Was the task successful?

Were there unexpected events or findings?

If the task was repeated, what could be improved?

Check what was found in the *Context* folder when reviewing!

Chapter 11: The *Mission End* tool-sheet

Reviewing the whole mission

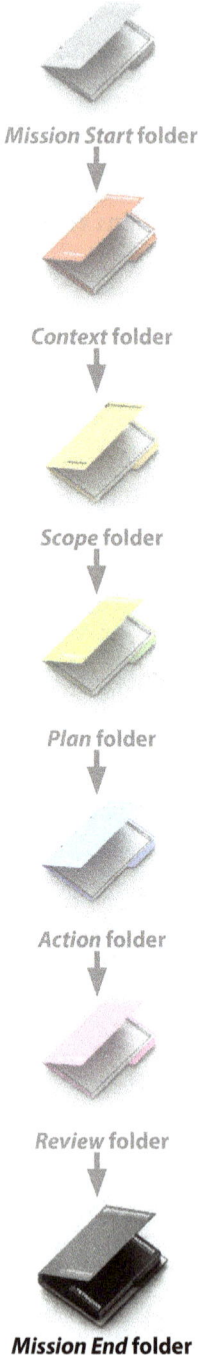

CHANGE→MAPPING
CONNECTING BUSINESS TOOLS TO MANAGE CHANGE

Mission Start folder

↓

Context folder

↓

Scope folder

↓

Plan folder

↓

Action folder

↓

Review folder

↓

Mission End folder

Once all the scopes of action have been completed, through planning, enacting the plans and reviewing them then the mission itself is reviewed.

Was the overall mission successful?

What was learnt by doing the mission and what could be done better? The *Mission End* tool-sheet works in a similar way to a *Review* tool-sheet. The first part looks at the enactment of the mission, while the second looks at the outcome of the mission.

Is the mission considered finished or will it become linked to other missions. Once this is done then the basic mission is then completed.

How to use the tool-sheet

General instructions

This tool-sheet is designed to be used by a small team of 4-12 **Explorers*** to capture ideas, information and insights during a mission. A **Pathfinder** will make sure the Explorers stay on the task, while allowing unexpected insights to occur.

An **Observer** will note down all the teams findings on the tool-sheet and additional paper if required.

The tool-sheet has a general information section which is used to identify the issue, mission and the tool-sheet itself.

It is recommended to review what happened during the **whole mission** to see what can be learnt.

Each section of the tool-sheet with circles asks the team to review the exploration or resolution of the mission.

The circles are not meant to be answered in any order, but rather start conversations.

The questions in the circles are not meant to cover every possible question, but rather the team can add their own context specific questions to the generic questions.

Once the review of the entire mission has been completed, the team will need to decide if the issue has been explored or resolved to everyone's satisfaction. If not then a **Linked mission** may be required, see page 36 for details.

*See page 12 about the roles in Change-mapping.

To show how the tool-sheets are used on the left one is filled in with a worked example. On the right is a blank version which can be photocopied for your own projects.

To effectively use the Mission end tool-sheet copies of **every** tool-sheet used in the mission will be required.

Mission End basic tool-sheet

CHANGE→MAPPING
CONNECTING BUSINESS TOOLS TO MANAGE CHANG

General information

Mission identification:
Shimrin/0001/2.2.22/new exhibition stand enquiry
Sheet identification:
Shimrin/0001/2.2.22/new exhibition stand enquiry, Mission End basic tool-sheet
The issue is:
Marketing manager believes we should invest in a new exhibition stand.
Our mission was:
To confirm to the board whether we should invest in a new exhibition stand.

How did the enactment of the entire mission proceed? Was there...

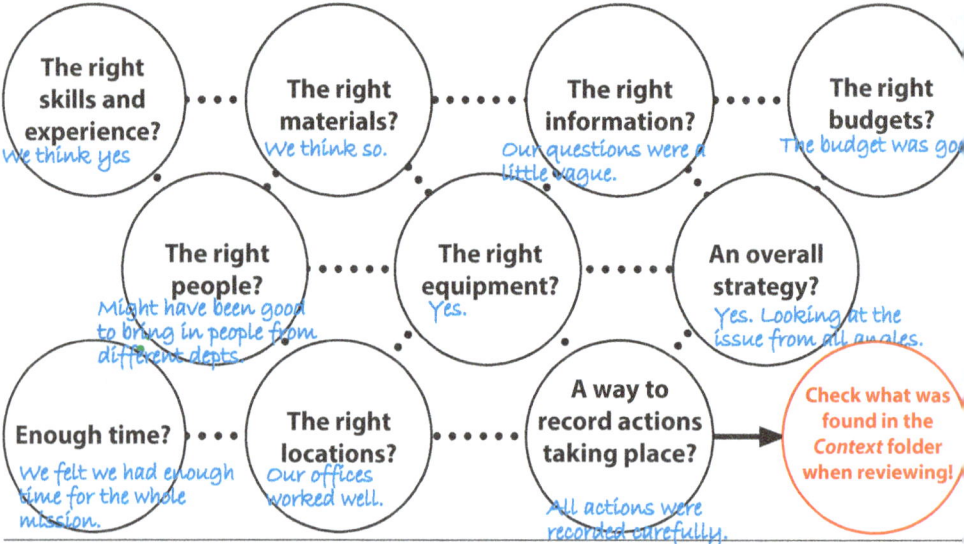

The right skills and experience?
We think yes

The right materials?
We think so.

The right information?
Our questions were a little vague.

The right budgets?
The budget was go[od]

The right people?
Might have been good to bring in people from different depts.

The right equipment?
Yes.

An overall strategy?
Yes. Looking at the issue from all angles.

Enough time?
We felt we had enough time for the whole mission.

The right locations?
Our offices worked well.

A way to record actions taking place?
All actions were recorded carefully.

Check what was found in the *Context* folder when reviewing!

What was the outcome of the mission?

What was learnt by doing the mission?
We found that our we now have a solid business case for investing in a new exhibition stand, rather than just rushing into investment.

Was the mission successful?
We felt it was as we have a better understanding ready to hand to the board about exhibition stands.

Were there unexpected events or findings?
The mission highlighted an unexpected area about how we store data and our industry regulation. We may to separate missions to find out more.

If the mission was repeated, what could be improved?
We would bring in a wider range of skills and experiences into the mission

What happens next?
If the board decid[e] to invest in a new stand based on this missions findings we will run al[l] inked mission to find out how to desig[n] and invest in a new exhibition stand.

Mission End basic tool-sheet

General information

Mission identification:

Sheet identification:

The issue is:

Our mission was:

How did the enactment of the entire mission proceed? Was there...

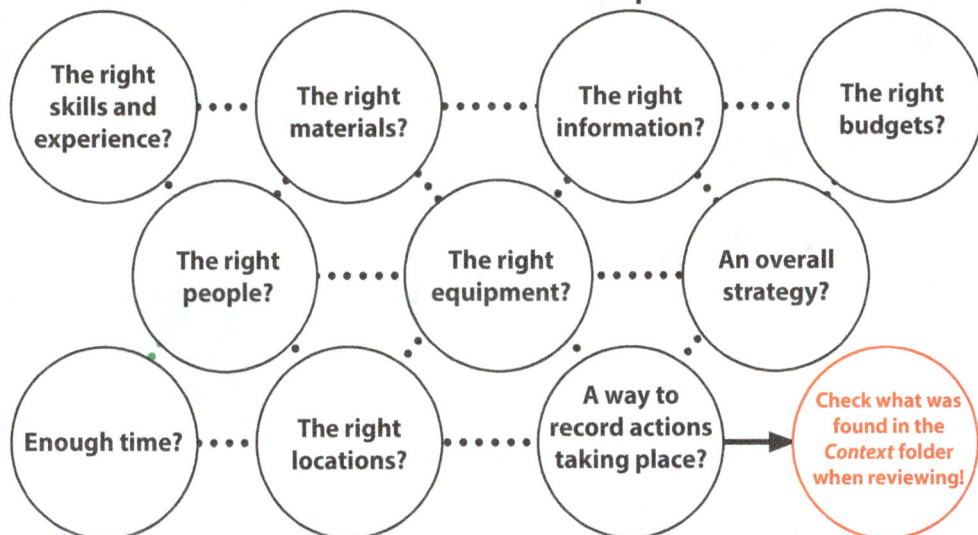

The right skills and experience? · · · The right materials? · · · · · The right information? · · · · The right budgets?

The right people? · · · · · The right equipment? · · · · · · An overall strategy?

Enough time? · · · The right locations? · · · · · A way to record actions taking place? → **Check what was found in the *Context* folder when reviewing!**

What was the outcome of the mission?

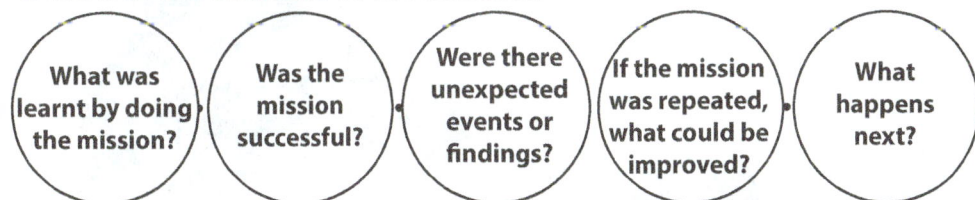

What was learnt by doing the mission? · Was the mission successful? · Were there unexpected events or findings? · If the mission was repeated, what could be improved? · What happens next?

Part 3:
Advanced *Change-mapping* in brief

An overview of how *Change-mapping* can be used to explore or resolve change issues of larger size and complexity

Chapter 12: *Running larger and more complex missions*

Change-mapping in use with larger and more complex issues

In depth

The examples shown here are a brief introduction to larger and more complex missions to map issues affected by change.
These types of missions and others will be discussed in greater depth with detailed diagrams and tool-sheets in the companion book:
Advanced Change-mapping.

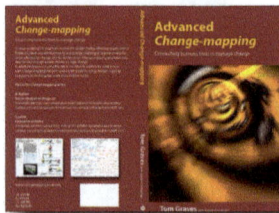

The main focus of this book has been to introduce *Change-mapping* to an organisation which has never used *Change-mapping* before.
But *Change-mapping* is not limited to simple small-scale issues. The same methods can be used for progressively larger and more complex issues. This chapter shows in brief how this can work. New specialised roles are also introduced. These mostly work by sharing information *across* missions and can also be of great benefit in smaller missions, not just larger and more complex missions.

An important note

Scaling the map

In simple missions the whole *Change-mapping* map with the coloured folders was shown. As the missions increase in size and complexity a whole mission is shown as one folder with the symbol '**Φ**'. Within that folder are all the coloured folders for that mission. This stops the map becoming too cluttered.

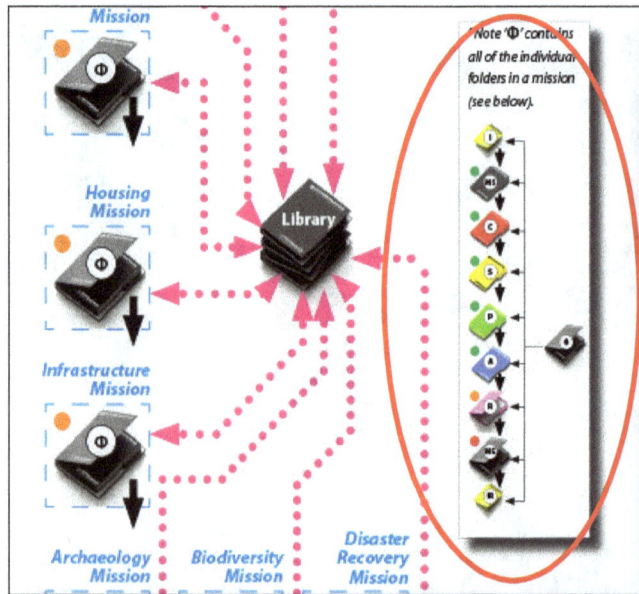

How to run scaled up missions
Introducing Coordinators

In depth
Coordinators work in a similar way to Librarians in that they retrieve, store and redistribute information gathered by the Explorers. The difference is that Librarians retrieve, store and distribute *all information*, while Coordinators can fine tune *when and what information* is sent and to who. For small missions a Librarian is most probably sufficient. But when large amounts of people and information require time sensitive information then a coordinator could prove very useful.
Coordination in Change-mapping has similarities with logistics, as that deals with the same types of issues. https://en.wikipedia.org/wiki/Logistics

Scaled up missions are a collection of missions which need to share information to achieve a common purpose. An example (*see right*) might be an aircraft manufacturer who designs and manufactures aircraft made up of thousands of parts. Each part will need to be designed, manufactured, tested and assembled in a certain order. All these missions will need to be coordinated with each other to avoid missed deadlines. The *Coordinator* becomes vital now by making sure that up to date information gets to the right people at the right time.

30 minute exercise
"Juggling a set of missions"
This exercise looks at setting the importance of one mission of another. If one person attempts to juggle one ball (which represents a mission) then it should be very easy.
Next try juggling two balls (missions) this again shouldn't be too difficult. But how about five balls at the same time.
For most untrained people this should prove very difficult so one option can be to have an expert help or to have five people sharing the load.
How might you decide what is important and who it is important to? How would you react to rapidly changing information and how would you get it to the right people at the right time?

An example of a set of scaled up missions
In this example getting the right information to the right people at the right time is critical.

Key
- Mission in-progress
- Completed mission
- Information flow
- Issue raised
- An ongoing mission*
- Issue explored or resolved

Note 'Φ' contains all of the individual folders in a mission (see below).

How to run large scale missions
Introducing Architects

In depth
Architects or Enterprise architects are often used by large organisations.
In simple terms they treat an organisation as a system and try to make all parts of work together efficiently. https://en.wikipedia.org/wiki/Enterprise_architecture
As missions increase in size and complexity they can help keep focus on the Big Picture without bias to one part of the organisation.
Another point of note is the difference between so called TAME and WICKED problems. In broad terms a TAME problem has a definite solution such as in maths while a WICKED problem is significantly harder to solve because as it is solved it can reveal other problems. More about these can be found at http://en.wikipedia.org/wiki/Wicked_problem

The diagram (*see right*) shows a large amount of missions all at different sizes, complexity and completion. Managing this amount of missions calls for a new role: the *Architect*. The *Architect* would, with a team of *Librarians* and *Coordinators* guide the whole set of missions to an end goal.
We could imagine all these missions having to work together so that a city could prosper while serving all its inhabitants.
An *Architect* would function in similar ways to a *Pathfinder* except guiding a set of missions rather than just one mission.

30 minute exercise
"A city sized mission"
In a highly simplified exercise, imagine that you and your team have to run a collection of missions to keep a city running effectively. How might you divide up what needs to be done. Would you have one person in control of everything or a network of people in control. How would you stop bias in one part, for example sanitation?
The aim of the exercise is to briefly imagine how you might tackle an extremely large and complex set of missions.

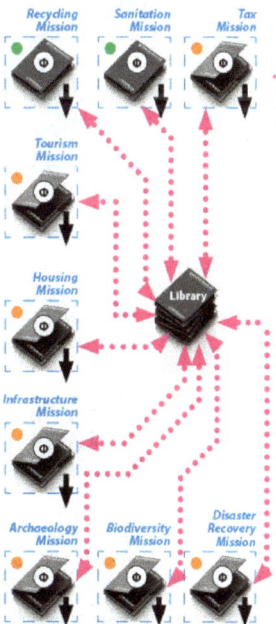

An example of a large scale mission
This mission is made up of multiple missions all working to a common objective.

Key
- Mission in-progress
- Completed mission
- Information flow
- Issue raised
- An ongoing mission*
- Issue explored or resolved

Note 'Φ' contains all of the individual folders in a mission (see below).

This chapter introduces more advanced parts of Change-mapping.

How to run parallel missions
Introducing Librarians and the Library

In depth
Waterfall* is a business tool which breaks projects into sequential parts. One advantage is clear distinctions between the stages of a project, but a disadvantage is that it can be hard to change parts once a stage has finished.

*https://en.wikipedia.org/wiki/ Waterfall_model

Agile** is another business tool which allows great flexibility in projects and communication. But sometimes *Agile* projects can lack direction and ignore disciplines from other proven business models.

**https://en.wikipedia.org/wiki/Agile_ software_development#Criticism

Parallel *Change-mapping* missions work the same way as regular *Change-mapping* missions. Teams explore or resolve issues using tool-sheets. The only difference is that they share information between each other as they proceed through their missions. In the diagram *(right)* we see two missions with different issues and at different stages sharing information.
A *Librarian* and library can be of great benefit in these situations as they can make sure that information is available to everyone that requires it.

30 minute exercise
"Setting up a Library for better information sharing"
In this exercise look at how you typically share information between teams and projects. Do you favour a **Waterfall*** approach or an **Agile**** approach to managing projects. How do you tackle rapidly changing information halfway through a project?
Change-mapping uses a combination of **Waterfall** and **Agile** by a continuous stream of information supplied by the Observers to the Library where it is redistributed to other Observers. How might you set up an information sharing method? Would it be every hour, day, week for example? What would be the best way to categorise the information?

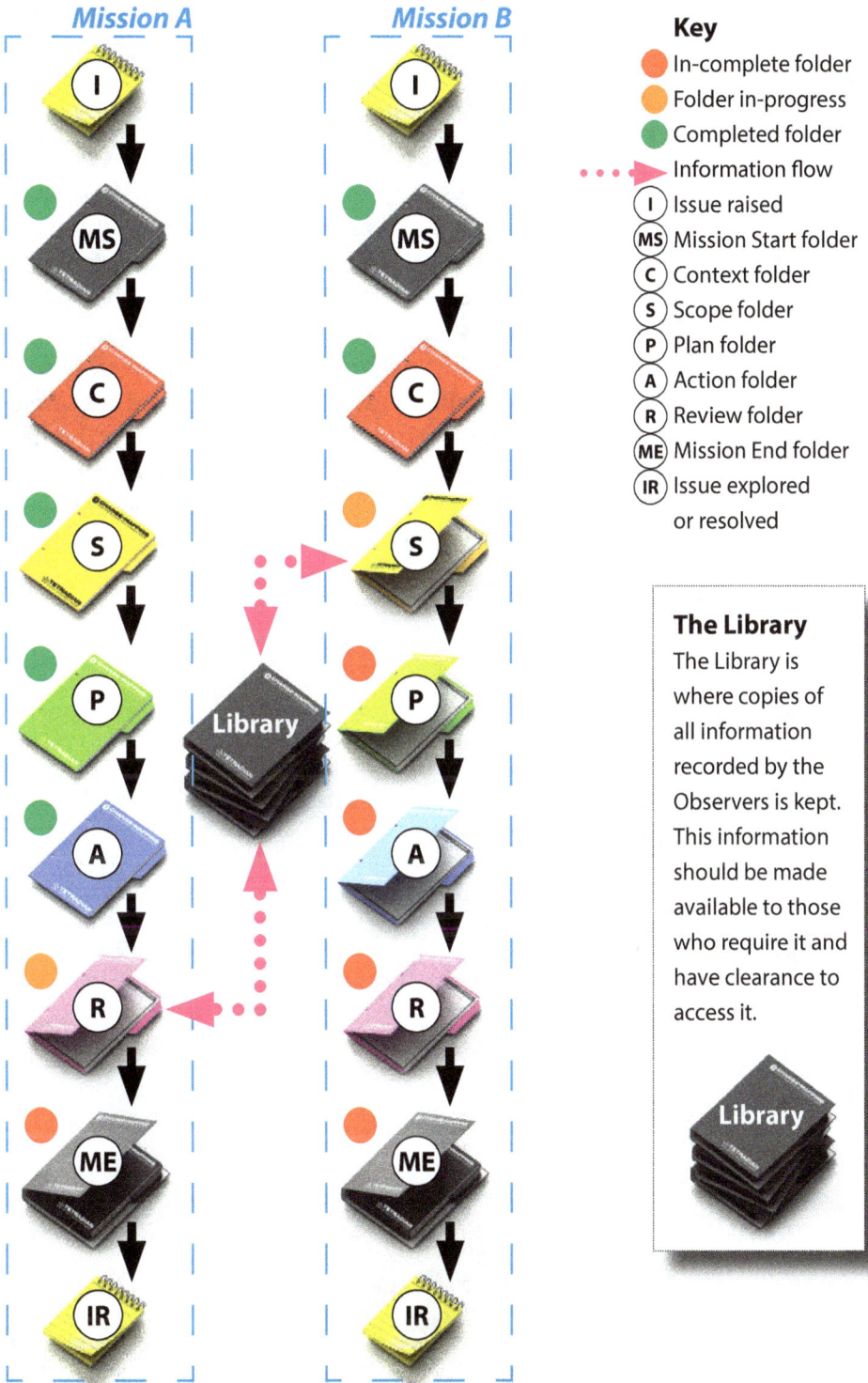

Key

- 🔴 In-complete folder
- 🟠 Folder in-progress
- 🟢 Completed folder
- •••➤ Information flow
- (I) Issue raised
- (MS) Mission Start folder
- (C) Context folder
- (S) Scope folder
- (P) Plan folder
- (A) Action folder
- (R) Review folder
- (ME) Mission End folder
- (IR) Issue explored or resolved

The Library

The Library is where copies of all information recorded by the Observers is kept. This information should be made available to those who require it and have clearance to access it.

An example of a Parallel mission
In this example one mission explores improving the organisation's IT infrastructure while at the same time another mission explores the organisation's energy usage.

How to run scaled up missions
Introducing Coordinators

In depth
Coordinators work in a similar way to Librarians in that they retrieve, store and redistribute information gathered by the Explorers. The difference is that Librarians retrieve, store and distribute **all information**, while Coordinators can fine tune **when and what information** is sent and to who. For small missions a Librarian is most probably sufficient. But when large amounts of people and information require time sensitive information then a coordinator could prove very useful.

Coordination in Change-mapping has similarities with logistics, as that deals with the same types of issues. *https://en.wikipedia.org/wiki/Logistics*

Scaled up missions are a collection of missions which need to share information to achieve a common purpose. An example *(see right)* might be an aircraft manufacturer who designs and manufacturers aircraft made up of thousands of parts. Each part will need to be designed,manufactured, tested and assembled in a certain order. All these missions will need to be coordinated with each other to avoid missed deadlines. A *Coordinator* becomes vital now by making sure that up to date information gets to the right people at the right time.

30 minute exercise
"Juggling a set of missions"
This exercise looks at setting the importance of one mission of another. If one person attempts to juggle one ball *(which represents a mission)* then it should be easy.
Next try juggling two balls *(missions)* this again shouldn't be too difficult. But how about five balls at the same time?
For most untrained people this should prove very difficult so one option can be to have an expert help or to have five people sharing the load.
How might you decide what is important and who it is important to? How would you react to rapidly changing information and how would you get it to the right people at the right time?

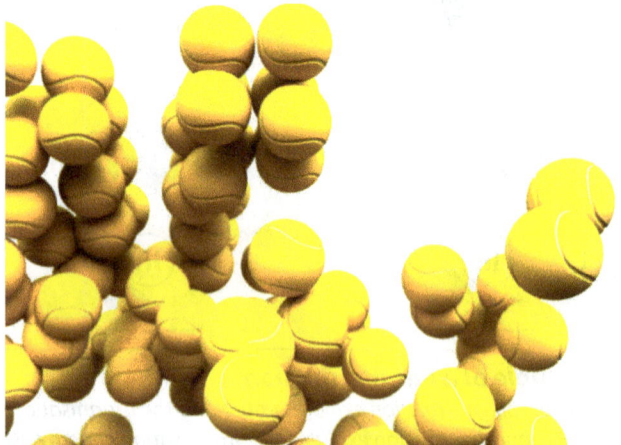

Key

- 🟠 Mission in-progress
- 🟢 Completed mission
- ⬤▶ Information flow
- Ⓘ Issue raised
- Ⓕ An ongoing mission*
- ⒤ᴿ Issue explored or resolved

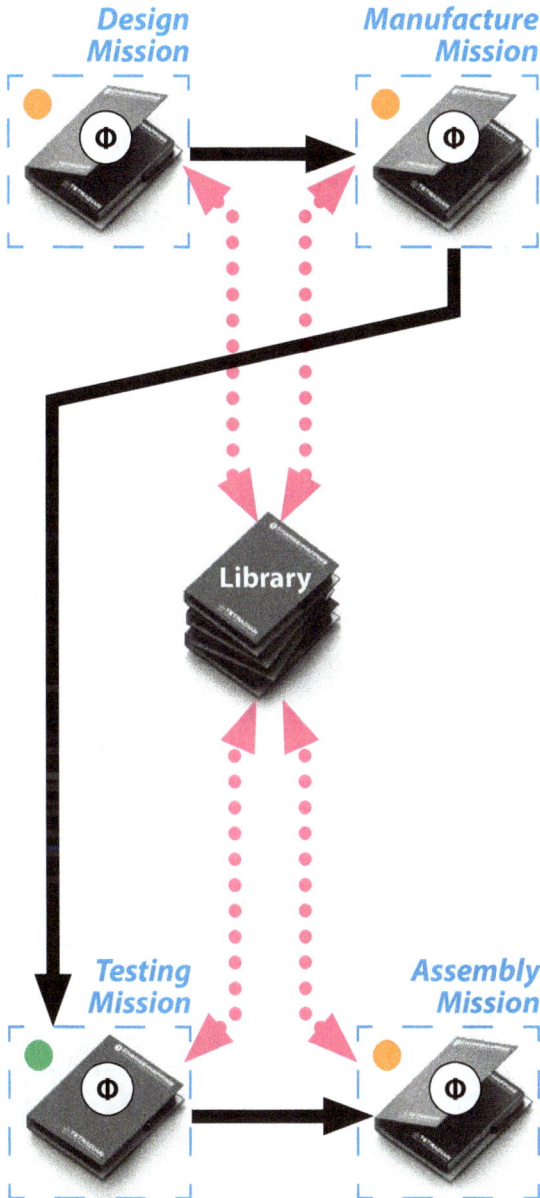

*Note 'Φ' contains all of the individual folders in a mission (see below).

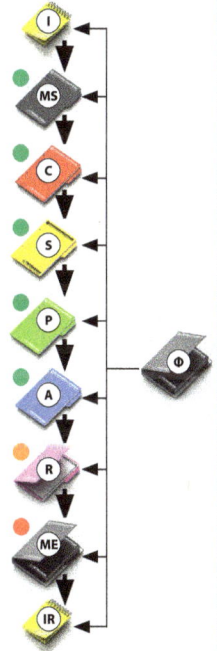

An example of a set of scaled up missions

In this example getting the right information to the right people at the right time is critical.

How to run large scale missions
Introducing Architects

In depth
Architects or Enterprise architects are often used by large organisations.
In simple terms they treat an organisation as a system and try to make all parts of work together efficiently. *https://en.wikipedia.org/ wiki/Enterprise_architecture* As missions increase in size and complexity they can help keep focus on the Big Picture without bias to one part of the organisation. Another point of note is the difference between so called **TAME** and **WICKED** problems. In broad terms a TAME problem has a definite solution such as in maths while a WICKED problem that is significantly harder to solve because as it is solved it can reveal other problems. More about these can be found at *https://en.wikipedia.org/ wiki/Wicked_problem*

The diagram *(see right)* shows a large amount of missions all at different sizes, complexity and completion. Managing this amount of missions calls for a new role: the *Architect*. The *Architect* would, with a team of *Librarians* and *Coordinators* guide the whole set of missions to an end goal. We could imagine all these missions having to work together so that a city could prosper while serving all its inhabitants.
An *Architect* would function in similar ways to a *Pathfinder* except guiding a set of missions rather than just one mission.

30 minute exercise
"A city sized mission"
In a highly simplified exercise, imagine that you and your team have to run a collection of missions to keep a city running effectively. How might you divide up what needs to be done. Would you have one person in control of everything or a network of people in control. How would you stop bias in one part, for example sanitation?
The aim of the exercise is to briefly imagine how you might tackle an extremely large and complex set of missions.

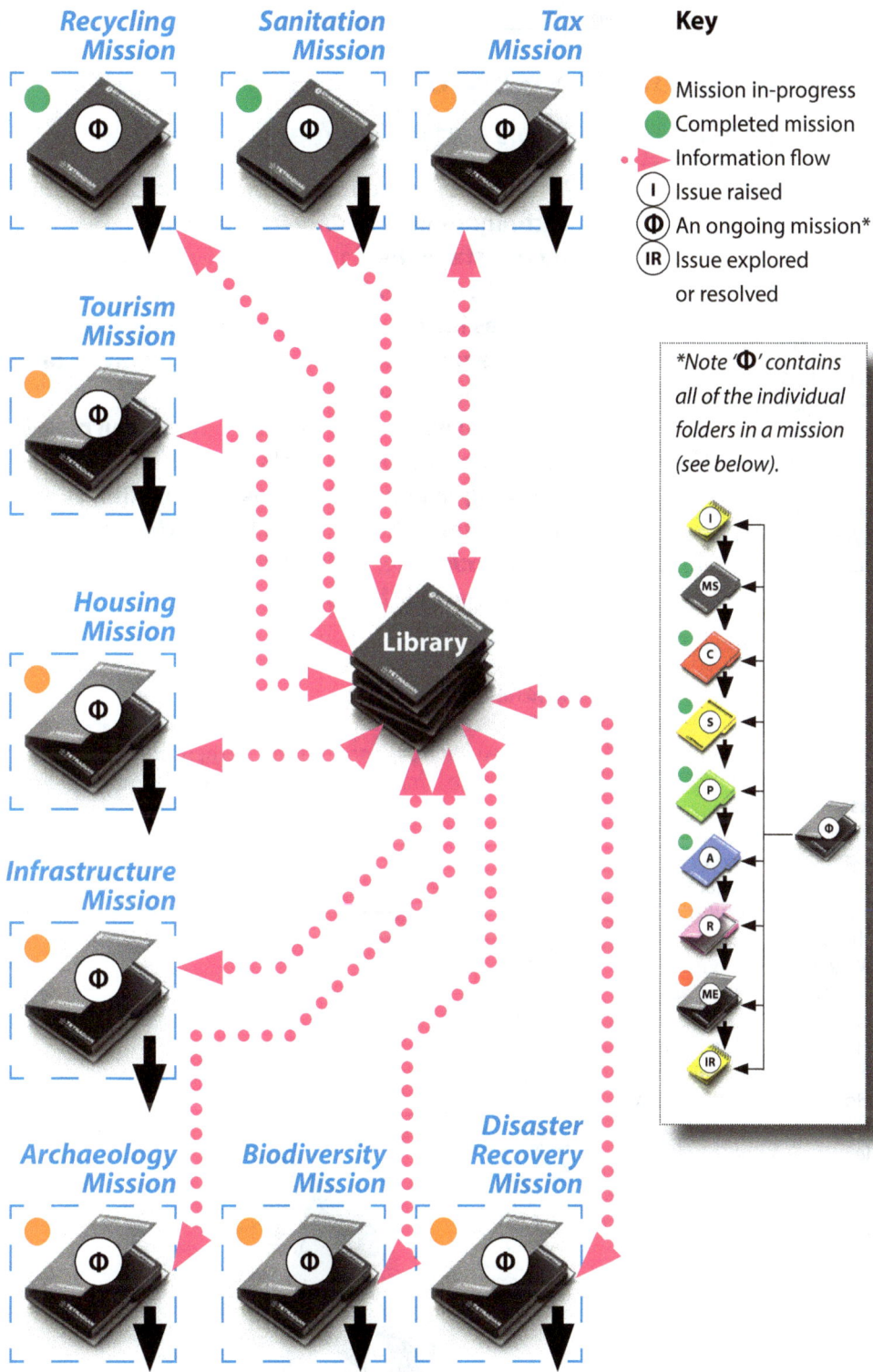

Key

- 🟠 Mission in-progress
- 🟢 Completed mission
- •••▶ Information flow
- Ⓘ Issue raised
- Φ An ongoing mission*
- ⒾⓇ Issue explored or resolved

*Note 'Φ' contains all of the individual folders in a mission (see below).

Recycling Mission

Sanitation Mission

Tax Mission

Tourism Mission

Housing Mission

Infrastructure Mission

Archaeology Mission

Biodiversity Mission

Disaster Recovery Mission

Library

An example of a large scale mission
This mission is made up of multiple missions all working to a common objective.

Chapter 13: Getting more out of *Change-mapping*

Using more advanced tools and techniques

In depth
Some general hints
and tips:

It can sometimes become confusing where you are inside a mission.
Which is why it is vital to use the *Mission Start* basic tool-sheet 2 of 2
(See page 66).
This acts as a map of the mission so you can see what you have done and what still needs to be done.

When running missions always look for assumptions.
Why are you doing this? It can be easy to get swept up with the excitement of a plan, but always question the plan.

Make sure that your lessons learnt are easy to find.
Having reviews is pointless if no one learns from them. How would another team benefit from what you learnt six months before? Is it scribbled on a bit of paper at the bottom of a drawer...

This chapter describes in brief two more advanced techniques used in *Change-mapping*.

By this stage the simplified tool-sheets will start to limit your missions. The simplified tool-sheets acted as introduction to Change-mapping and so have generic questions which should give a *broad* picture of *any* issue.

But if you want more detail, then you can *plug-in* more context specific tools.

This *plug-in* approach allows huge flexibility and great detail, while still you to see where you are in the *overall* issue, without becoming too focused on one part of the issue.

Specialised exercises
General instructions
In this chapter are a set of small exercises which tackle more advanced parts of *Change-mapping*. These are best done once you are familiar with missions, as they build on previous exercises shown in the book.

10 minute exercise
"A Nested mission to promote our pizzas."
In this exercise we take the example *(see right)* and recreate that mission and *Nested mission*. The idea of *Nested missions* can be a bit confusing at first. They work in some ways a bit like another *Scope* folder but they can be created in any folder, except the *Action* folder *(see page 28).*
They work in a similar fashion to *Preselected* tool-sheets *(see left).*

Using existing tools within *Change-mapping*

How to integrate the tools you know in missions

In depth

When a team has tried to answer a question using the basic tool-sheet but they have not obtained enough detail then their next option is to use a *Existing tool*.

If using a *Existing tool* doesn't give enough information then they can try a *Nested mission* (see page 114).

Another book in this series:

Tools for Change-mapping will look at a selection of tools designed by the author and others such as *Holomap, SEMPER, SCAN and SCORE*.

In addition it will look at integrating other tools such as the *Four Ps, GANTT charts* and others.

Within a mission to explore or resolve an issue the basic tool-sheets may just not give enough detail. The basic tool-sheets act as simple conversation starters, but if more detail is required, what next? The next option the team has is to use an *Existing tool* to answer that question. Choosing **which** *Existing tool* to use, is outside the scope of this book (see left). As a **rough** guide any strategy tool would be used in the *Context* folder, any planning tool would be used in the *Mission Start, Scope* and *Plan* folders. Any review tool would be used in the *Review* and *Mission End* folders.

10 minute exercise

"using the Four Ps to promote a new watch"

In this exercise we take a well known business tool and use it within a mission to promote a new watch.

The mission (see right) acts like typical missions, but instead of just using tool-sheets use the *Four Ps* as well to explore the issue.

For more information about using existing tools in *Change-mapping* see bottom left.

An example of a mission with an Existing tool
In this example during a mission the team have not been able to answer a question, so they use an *Existing tool* while inside the *Scope* folder.

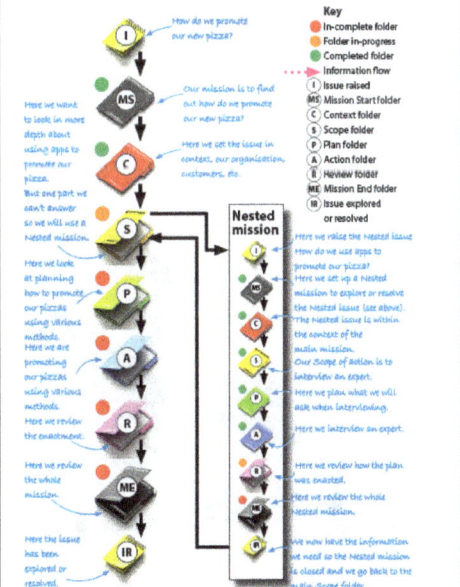

Nested Missions

Going into more detail to answer questions

In depth

Nested missions tend to be used when the team has tried to answer a question using the basic tool-sheet but the *Preselected tool-sheet (see page 112)*. This is a simple list of tools which have worked for others in similar circumstances. But sometimes without assistance these tool-sheets can still leave the question unanswered.

A *Nested mission* creates a new issue "We can't answer *this* question" and creates a small mission to explore or resolve *just* that question. Preselected tools offer less customisation but tend to be faster to use.

Nested missions offer huge customisation but are slower to use as they will need much more setting up. This is why the Preselected tool is given as the first option (see page 58) and Nested missions are given as the last option.

When running a mission the team will attempt to answer questions on the tool-sheets. If they can't then they can try using a *Nested mission*. A *Nested mission (see right)* works exactly the same as a regular mission, except that is exploring or resolving one question about the issue, rather than the whole issue. For example if a team has the issue "How do we promote our new pizza?" they might run a *Nested mission* which looks only at how to promote the new pizza using an app. *Nested missions* act as highly customisable tool-sheets to explore or resolve a specific issue.

10 minute exercise

"A Nested mission to promote our pizza."

In this exercise we take the example (see right) and recreate that mission and *Nested mission*. The idea of *Nested missions* can be a bit confusing at first. They work in some ways a bit like another *Scope* folder but they can be created in any folder, except the *Action* folder (see page 28). They work in a similar fashion to *Preselected* tool-sheets (see left).

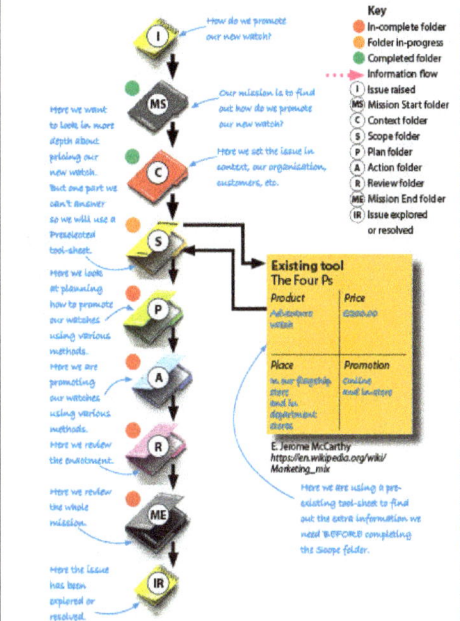

An example of a mission with a Nested mission
In this example during a mission the team have not been able to answer a question, even with a more detailed pre-selected tool. So they use a Nested mission to answer the question.

This chapter looks in brief at some advanced Change-mapping techniques.

Using existing tools within *Change-mapping*

How to integrate the tools you know in missions

In depth

When a team has tried to answer a question using the basic tool-sheet but they have not obtained enough detail then their next option is to use a **Existing tool**.
If using a **Existing tool** doesn't give enough information then they can try a **Nested mission** *(see page 114).*

Another book in this series: **Tools for Change-mapping** will look at a selection of tools designed by the author and others such as **Holomap, SEMPER, SCAN and SCORE.**
In addition it will look at integrating other tools such as the **Four Ps, GANTT charts** and others.

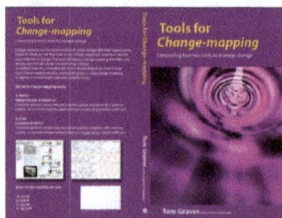

Within a mission to explore or resolve an issue the basic tool-sheets may just not give enough detail. The basic tool-sheets act as simple conversation starters, but if more detail is required, what next? The next option the team has is to use an *Existing tool* to answer that question. Choosing **which** *Existing tool* to use, is outside the scope of this book *(see left)*. As a **rough** guide any strategy tool would be used in the *Context* folder, any planning tool would be used in the *Mission Start, Scope* and *Plan* folders. Any review tool would be used in the *Review* and *Mission End* folders.

10 minute exercise

"Using the Four Ps to promote a new watch"
In this exercise we take a well known business tool and use it within a mission to promote a new watch.
The mission *(see right)* acts like typical missions, but instead of just using tool-sheets use the **Four Ps** as well to explore the issue.
For more information about using existing tools in *Change-mapping* see bottom left.

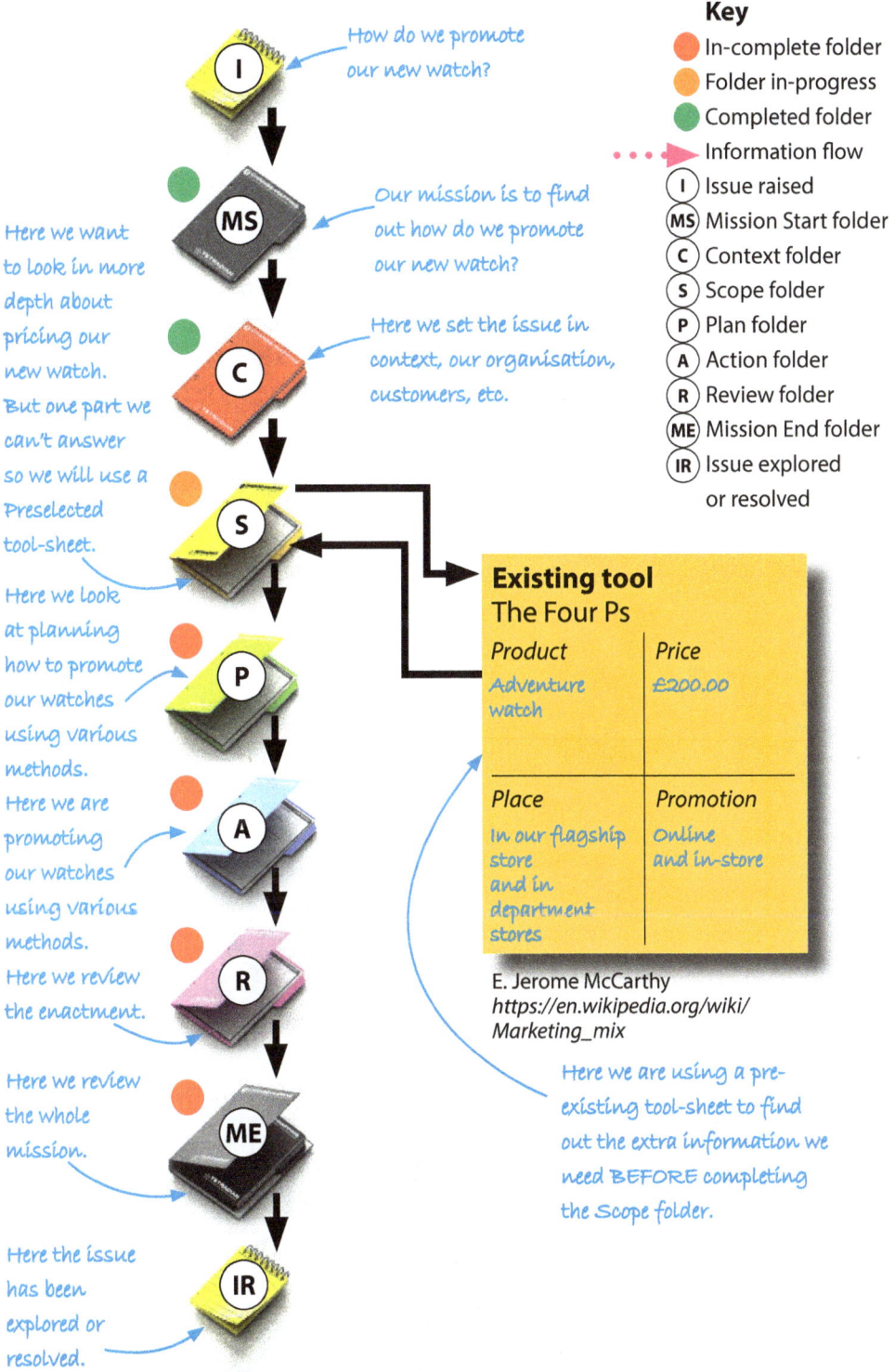

Key
- 🔴 In-complete folder
- 🟠 Folder in-progress
- 🟢 Completed folder
- ● ● ● ▶ Information flow
- (I) Issue raised
- (MS) Mission Start folder
- (C) Context folder
- (S) Scope folder
- (P) Plan folder
- (A) Action folder
- (R) Review folder
- (ME) Mission End folder
- (IR) Issue explored or resolved

How do we promote our new watch?

Our mission is to find out how do we promote our new watch?

Here we want to look in more depth about pricing our new watch. But one part we can't answer so we will use a Preselected tool-sheet.

Here we set the issue in context, our organisation, customers, etc.

Here we look at planning how to promote our watches using various methods.

Here we are promoting our watches using various methods.

Here we review the enactment.

Here we review the whole mission.

Here the issue has been explored or resolved.

Existing tool
The Four Ps

Product	Price
Adventure watch	£200.00

Place	Promotion
In our flagship store and in department stores	Online and in-store

E. Jerome McCarthy
https://en.wikipedia.org/wiki/Marketing_mix

Here we are using a pre-existing tool-sheet to find out the extra information we need BEFORE completing the Scope folder.

An example of a mission with an Existing tool
In this example during a mission the team have not been able to answer a question, so they use an Existing tool while inside the Scope folder.

Nested Missions

Going into more detail to answer questions

In depth

Nested missions tend to be used when the team has tried to answer a question using the basic tool-sheet. Their next option is to use an **Existing tool** *(see page 112)*.

But sometimes without assistance these **Existing tools** can still leave the question unanswered.

A **Nested mission** creates a new issue *"We can't answer this question"* and creates a small mission to explore or resolve **just** that question. **Existing tools** offer less customisation but tend to be faster to use.

Nested missions offer huge customisation but are slower to use as they will need much more setting up. This is why the Preselected tool is given as the first option *(see page 58)* and Nested missions are given as the last option.

When running a mission the team will attempt to answer questions on the tool-sheets. If they can't then they can try using a *Nested mission*.
A *Nested mission (see right)* works exactly the same as a regular mission, except that is exploring or resolving one question about the issue, rather than the whole issue. For example if a team has the issue"*How do we promote our new pizza?*" they might run a *Nested mission* which looks only at how to promote the new pizza using an app. *Nested missions* act as highly customisable ways to explore or resolve a specific issue.

10 minute exercise
"A Nested mission to promote our pizzas."

In a simple exercise run a mission to explore how to promote a new line of pizzas. If we imagine that using social media was suggested, then you will run a *Nested mission* which is focused **only** on using social media to promote pizzas. What you find in that *Nested mission* will then be used in the main mission.

Key

- 🔴 In-complete folder
- 🟠 Folder in-progress
- 🟢 Completed folder
- ···▶ Information flow
- (I) Issue raised
- (MS) Mission Start folder
- (C) Context folder
- (S) Scope folder
- (P) Plan folder
- (A) Action folder
- (R) Review folder
- (ME) Mission End folder
- (IR) Issue explored or resolved

How do we promote our new pizza?

Our mission is to find out how do we promote our new pizza?

Here we set the issue in context, our organisation, customers, etc.

Here we want to look in more depth about using apps to promote our pizza.

But one part we can't answer so we will use a Nested mission.

Here we look at planning how to promote our pizzas using various methods.

Here we are promoting our pizzas using various methods.

Here we review the enactment.

Here we review the whole mission.

Here the issue has been explored or resolved.

Nested mission

Here we raise the Nested issue How do we use apps to promote our pizza?

Here we set up a Nested mission to explore or resolve the Nested issue (see above). The Nested issue is within the context of the main mission.

Our Scope of action is to interview an expert.

Here we plan what we will ask when interviewing.

Here we interview an expert.

Here we review how the plan was enacted.

Here we review the whole Nested mission.

We now have the information we need so the Nested mission is closed and we go back to the main Scope folder.

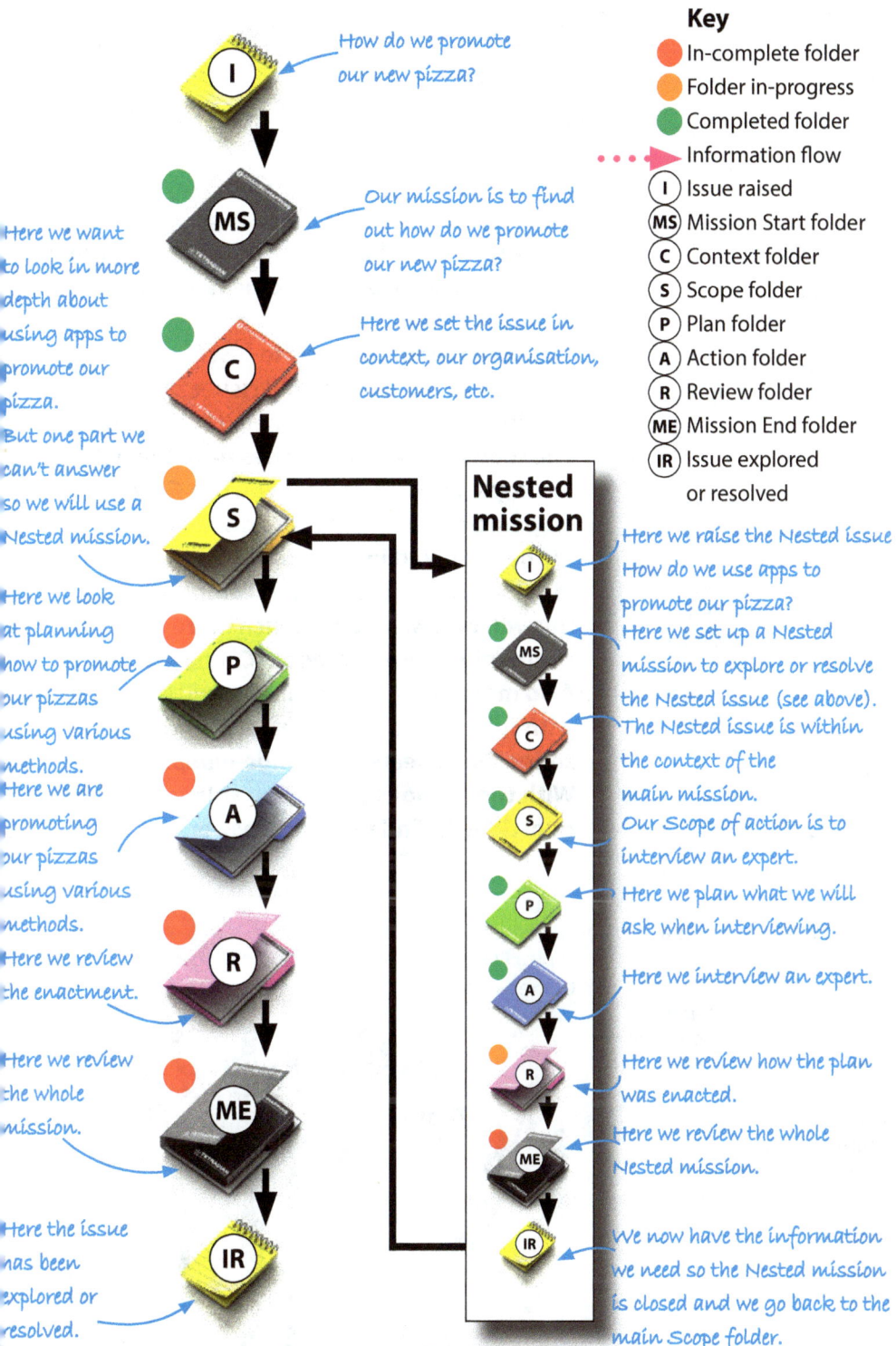

An example of a mission with a Nested mission

In this example during a mission the team have not been able to answer a question, so they use a Nested mission to answer the question.

Chapter 14: What to do next?

Using more advanced tools and techniques

In depth

This book contains a small amount of theory and useable tool-sheets so that you can start to explore or resolve issues affected by change. These should be sufficient for simple issues. When tackling more complex issues the same techniques apply, but how the information found is stored and distributed becomes more critical. When designing the book and Change-mapping itself everything was tested without computer systems. The logic being that if it worked on paper first then it should be possible to adapt it to working as a program or an app.
It is most likely that as the issues become complex that computer systems will be needed to share and store information.
This will be discussed further in the companion books.

This book has introduced a new way to explore or resolve issues affected by change.
It is hoped that the reader will work through the book and exercises to become familiar with how everything works.
Then the reader can start to test how *Change-mapping* could work on old issues before cautiously using it on live small scale issues.
The tool-sheets and exercises have been designed to simple to use, but once you use *Change-mapping* you will find these quite limiting.
We have looked in brief in this book about missions for large scale and complex issues, this will be discussed in much more detail in the companion book '*Advanced Change-mapping*'.
Also more detailed tool-sheets will be described, with full instructions in the other book in the series '*Tool-sheets for Change-mapping*'.
With these books you will be able to ask the right questions to find the right answers.

A final note

Have a go!
Typically the best way to learn something is to have a go.
Gather a small team and have fun!

This book describes in brief Change-mapping, which is used to tackle issues affected by change.

www.ingramcontent.com/pod-product-compliance
Lightning Source LLC
Chambersburg PA
CBHW071204200326
41519CB00018B/5358